PYTHON CODING

FOR KIDS

A Beginner's Guide to Coding. Learn to Code with
Hands-On Projects and Examples. Master the Basics With
Fun and Interactive Exercises in 7 Days

Santos Ozoemena

Dedication

To my readers

This book is dedicated to you, passionate readers. You have been an unwavering source of support, encouragement, and inspiration throughout my journey as a writer. Your belief in me and your constant presence in my life has been instrumental in bringing this book to fruition.

You have always been there to listen to my ideas, provide valuable feedback, and lend a helping hand whenever I needed it. Your unwavering faith in my abilities has pushed me to strive for greatness and overcome the inevitable challenges that arise on the path of writing.

I am grateful for the countless hours you have spent reading my drafts, offering insightful suggestions, and cheering me on from the sidelines. Your honest and constructive criticism has helped shape this book into its best possible form.

Beyond your role as a dedicated supporter, you have been a true friend, offering love, laughter, and companionship. Your unwavering belief in me as a person has given me the confidence to pursue my dreams and embrace the vulnerability that comes with sharing my work.

This dedication is a testament to the profound impact you have had on my life and my writing. Your unwavering support has been the driving force behind my creativity and the reason I am able to share this book with the world today.

Thank you for your unwavering support, love, and belief in me. This book is dedicated to you with heartfelt gratitude and deep appreciation.

With love and appreciation,

Santos Ozoemena

Acknowledgment

I would like to express my heartfelt gratitude to all those who have contributed to the creation and publication of this book. Without their support, encouragement, and expertise, this endeavor would not have been possible.

First and foremost, I would like to thank my family for their unwavering love and support throughout this entire journey. Your belief in me and your constant encouragement has been the driving force behind my determination to see this project through. Thank you for always being there for me, cheering me on, and providing the necessary comfort and motivation to keep going.

I am deeply grateful to my friends and colleagues who have offered their valuable insights, feedback, and encouragement. Your enthusiasm for this project has been infectious, and I am fortunate to have such a supportive network of individuals who have believed in me and my work. Your constructive criticism and helpful suggestions have undoubtedly improved the quality of this book.

I extend my sincerest appreciation to my editor, Jacob Hause, whose keen eye and editorial expertise have polished this manuscript and elevated it to new heights. Your guidance, meticulous attention to detail, and commitment to excellence have been invaluable. I am truly grateful for the hours you dedicated to refining and shaping this book.

I would also like to acknowledge the contributions of the research assistants, proofreaders, and beta readers who generously volunteered their time and expertise. Your meticulousness and dedication in ensuring the accuracy and clarity of this book have been instrumental in its final form. Your commitment to the craft of writing and your willingness to lend a helping hand have my deepest gratitude.

Furthermore, I am indebted to the professionals in the publishing industry who have believed in this book and provided their support along the way. From agents to designers, marketers to distributors, each person has played a crucial role in bringing this work to the hands of readers. Thank you for your expertise, guidance, and commitment to making this book a reality.

Finally, I would like to express my appreciation to all the readers and supporters who have embraced my writing and given me the opportunity to share my ideas and stories. Your enthusiasm and encouragement fuel my passion as a writer, and I am grateful for the connection we have formed through the pages of this book.

To everyone mentioned above and to those whose names I may have unintentionally omitted, please accept my heartfelt thanks. Your contributions have left an indelible mark on this book, and I am humbled and grateful for your support.

With deepest gratitude,
Santos Ozoemena

Contents

Preface

As a Data Scientist and tech consultant, I have worked with some of the biggest names in the industry, including Disney, CVS, and T-Mobile. Through my experience in the tech industry, I have seen firsthand the importance of coding and how it is becoming an essential skill in today's digital world.

But coding doesn't have to be just for adults. Children can also learn to code, and it can be a fun and rewarding experience. That's why I decided to write Python Coding for Kids: A Beginner's Guide to Coding.

This book is designed to be an engaging and interactive way for kids to learn the fundamentals of coding, using the popular programming language, Python. With hands-on projects, interactive exercises, and fun examples, kids can learn to code in just 7 days.

Python is an excellent language for beginners because of its simplicity and readability, and it is widely used in various applications, including game development, data analysis, and web development. In this book, children will learn the basics of coding, such as how to use functions, variables, and data structures. They will also learn how to write their own code, debug programs, and create fun projects like games and quizzes.

The book is designed to be easy to understand and apply, with step-by-step instructions and clear explanations. It's also interactive, with plenty of exercises and activities to keep children engaged and motivated.

I hope that Python Coding for Kids will inspire children to pursue their curiosity in technology and set them on a path to becoming the next generation of tech innovators.

Introduction

I think everybody in this country should learn how to program a computer because it teaches you how to think. – Steve Jobs

Have you ever wondered what creating your own video game would be like? Well, if you have, this could be one reason for learning to code in python! And you don't need to remember long lines of code or information to make it good. Python is a language considered one of the easiest to learn and read. This means that you can become an ace at it in no time.

With this book, I will teach you how to start writing your own Python code and develop your programs. While this might not seem like a lot, you should know that python is becoming one of the most popular languages in the market. This means that you will soon have the knowledge that several professionals have—and that will make a difference in the future.

While you are reading, I will explain some of python's basic features and the most relevant functions you can perform. Each chapter will have practice exercises and a challenge (you can find the answers to these at the end of the book). This will help you learn the concepts more easily. Furthermore, by completing these practice tests, you will have opportunities to apply what you have seen, making it easier to remember.

Now, without further delay, let's start our lessons! Enjoy, and see you at the end.

Santos Ozoemena

A FREE GIFT TO OUR READERS

7 surprising beginner mistakes you should avoid as a beginner programmer downloadable guideline. This will set you on the right path to learning how to program.

santosbooks.com

Chapter 1: What is Python?

Python is a common programming language that is widely used around the world in various fields. One of the main reasons this language is used so much is because it is considered productive and fast, especially if you need to fix any mistakes. Another advantage is that it is easy to read, enabling you to quickly identify what each line of code will do without going through long and complicated structures. Finally, when you learn python, you will see several libraries with code possibilities and examples to help you develop faster and more efficiently.

Why Should You Learn Python?

Python is very easy to learn. When you compare it to other popular languages, you will see that its structure is more readable and the logic more comprehensive. This makes it the ideal language for a beginner to learn if they want to start developing programs. While other languages have different ways of writing the same thing, python is not as flexible, which makes it easier to get the "right code" without being confused (OpenSource, n.d.).

Another reason to learn python is that it will automatically clean up your program's memory for any code lines that are not used in a garbage collection process. This will make it easier to free up space in your computer and enable you to continue developing without worrying about getting rid of useless information. Last but not least, you will find an enormous quantity of communities dedicated to python on internet pages with which you can exchange ideas and code.

You want to know what those who program in python like to call themselves? Pythonistas! Yes! And now that you are learning python, you will soon become a Pythonista as well. Python is so amazing and captivating that as soon as you start studying it, you will see how cool it can be! And you know what the best part is? Most of the programs that you see or use have python in them!

Want to bet? Well, read on because, in the next section, I will give you a list of companies that use the technology. Check them out!

Companies That Use Python

Here is a list of five companies that use python in their software. Do you recognize any of them? Do you use any of them regularly? You might be surprised that some of them are built almost entirely with the language.

- **Spotify**: This music streaming company likes and uses python so much that they are one of the sponsors of a few Python events! Have you ever noticed how fast the service for the application is? Well, this is one of the main reasons why the company has decided to use Python: It makes the programs run fast and easy to collect and analyze information regarding what the users are listening to.

- **NASA**: Did you know that NASA uses python to build programs to send shuttles or astronauts to space? Can you imagine how cool that is? Because it is such a simple language, NASA adopted it to avoid making solutions too complicated when creating their programs. In addition, and this is very cool when you learn python, you can look on the company's webpage for NASA program code that is open to the public. If learning how the space giant operates is not fun, I don't know what is!

- **Google**: When researching for school, which search engine do you use? It is safe to say that most users will rely on Google, a huge company that uses a lot of python all around, but especially in one of their top products. Can you guess what it is? If you guessed YouTube, you are correct! The video website is almost all built-in python because it helps the company better control the content and its numbers. What is neat is that YouTube uses Python code to give you suggestions of

4

videos that you would like to see based on what you have seen before.

- **Uber**: When your parents call for an Uber, did you know they are using Python technology? That is because most of the platform's services are written using this coding language, along with a few others. Once again, this choice is because of the amazing volume of information the application deals with and because its customers expect fast service when searching for a ride.

- **Netflix**: Finally, the last company on our small list. Netflix uses python because of all the reasons you have already read about. If you think about all the services and information it needs to deal with, such as customer preferences, analyzing information, and being fast, you might understand why this is so. In addition to all these applications, the platform also applies python for its security features and to make it possible for you to watch from any device you want—the television, mobile phone, tablet, or computer. Netflix is such a huge user of python that they have their *own library* with codes and solutions that you can refer to if needed.

Of course, these are not the only applications that use python—several others are out there, such as Facebook, Instagram, Dropbox, and PayPal. I just wanted you to know how some of the companies you already know use the language and how valuable it is. Cool, right?

Why Learning Python Is for the Cool Kids Only

Apart from understanding all these companies are doing with python, learning it will also help you in several different areas. For example, learning how to code in python can help you with your studies since it will increase your concentration and focus. Practicing these skills will make it easier to concentrate on difficult tasks and any work that requires your full attention (The Real School, 2022).

Learning python will also help you practice your logic and early programming skills. If you enjoy computers and technology and believe they are important to know about in the future, the sooner you begin learning, the better! And what better way to start than with a simple and easy-to-understand language used by millions of people?

Lastly, and I saved the best for last, once you know how to program in python, you can start your own projects. This can include designing your own video game. There is even a feature in Minecraft, for example, which allows the users to program into the game to make it more personalized! In addition, you can sharpen your skills by playing a game called CodeCombat, where you will need to use Python code to solve missions. In the game, you can also access Trinket, which will show you some applications of python in real life and how to apply them to your routine (Tiwari, 2021).

Well, now that you know the basics of python, let's get to work! Installing Java on your computer is the first thing you will need to start programming. If you have trouble doing so, ask a parent or a guardian to help you with the instructions. Although the process is not hard to follow, having someone help you navigate through the computer folders and directories may prevent any mishaps from occurring.

Installing Python

In this section, you will learn how to download python for your computer. You will see the options for downloading if you have Windows, Linux, or macOS. The first thing you will need to do is go to the official Python page, python.org, and decide which version of python you want to download (it is now in the third version). Each version has several download options. Once you click on **downloads**, you will see a list of all the versions and the operating systems options for the most adequate download.

Installing Python on PC—Windows

The latest version of Python for Windows is 3.12 (this information will be seen right at the top of the page). If you have either Linux or Windows, you will select one of the available options by clicking on the link, which will take you directly to the download page. According to your operating system, you must choose between the 32- or 64-bit version. Once you have identified your computer's configuration, click on the corresponding link for a popup window to open and prompt the download of a zipped folder.

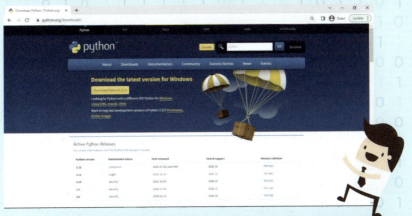

Once the folder is saved on your computer, decompress it and launch the installer. Leave the **Install launcher for all users** box, as well as the **Add Python 3.9 to Path** box checked. Next, you should click Install Now for the download process. Once the process is over, the dialogue box will change, and the message, **Setup was successful**, will appear on your screen. You have installed python on your machine, but it is always a good idea to check if everything went okay, so we will make sure it is there.

First, you should open the **cmd** prompt in the system and ask it to run **Python-V** to see if it is there. The window will open and the message that appears should show the version of Java installed. If this is what you see once you run the command, congratulations! You have successfully installed python and can now start using the program!

Installing Python on PC—Linux
If you are using Linux, here is something you will love to

know: This operating system already comes with python! Yes, you read it right. You do not need to download the program because it is already there. All you will need to do is check the version it contains to ensure that when you search for features and libraries, they match the version you are using. In addition, the installed version might not be the most recent version, so it is always best to double-check and upgrade if needed (Real Python, n.d.).

To identify the version of Python your Linux has, you will need to follow just a few simple steps. Go to the command terminal and type in the **$ python --version**. To check for versions 2 and 3, you will type in the following: **$ python2 --version** or **$ python3 --version** (Real Python, n.d.). The information should appear automatically. However, suppose you do not have the latest version. In that case, you will need to update it by using the following commands that, according to Arora (2021), will work in almost all Linux environments:

$ sudo add-apt-repository ppa:deadsnakes/ppa

$ sudo apt-get update

$ sudo apt-get install python3.7

Furthermore, according to Python Land (2023), if your Linux is either Ubuntu, Linux Mint, or Debian, you can also install the most recent version by using the following command in the prompt:

$ apt install python3 python-is-python3

Once you have done this, run the check again to ensure that the correct version is installed, and you are good to go!

Installing python on macOS

Search the internet for How to install python in macOS. You will see that several sites will tell you that the program already comes embedded in the operational system. However, the version that comes with it is Python 2.7, which was discontinued, and for this reason, it will only be available if your Mac version is between 10.8 and 12.3 (Yadav, 2022).

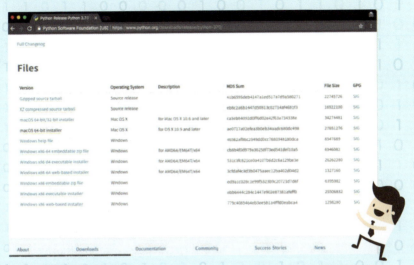

To check the version installed on your computer, go to the **Mac Launchpad** and type in the word **terminal** in the **search** field. Once the screen appears, Yadav (2022) instructs to type in the command:

Python --version

This will verify your computer's version, which should be version 2.7.18. The same commands you have seen on Linux should be used to also verify the possibility of version 3 being installed. Since there are newer versions of python you can use to download the package, you will once again need to go to the official python.org website and find the latest version to download. Click on the link, and once the download is finished, click Install to continue the process.

Once this process is done, a window will immediately appear on your screen with all the tools that have been downloaded. To check if the download was correctly completed, use the commands you have previously seen in the Mac Launchpad with the word terminal. This will confirm the version you have, and if it's correct, you are all set to start!

Using IDLE to Write Python Code

When you install python on your computer, it will also automatically install an application named IDLE. IDLE stands for Integrated Development and Learning Environment (a mouthful!), and it's an integrated development environment (IDE) that helps us write Python programs. Consider it an electronic notebook with a few more tools to assist us in writing, debugging, and running Python code. You'll need to launch IDLE to work in python—opening Python files directly won't work! In this program, you will write your code, run programs, and save your files. This will be your main tool to edit the code or interpret what you have written.

Run Your Program

Once Python and the IDLE are installed on your computer and you have checked and verified the installation information, you are ready to start. To begin writing your code, as we will see from now on, you must open the IDLE program so it can run. A new window will appear, and you will see information regarding the product on your screen. To open a new file to start developing, you must click on the **File** button and then on **New File**, which will open a blank page.

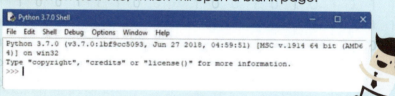

You are now ready and set to go! Prepared to begin learning how to code in python? Read on to start your lessons!

Chapter 2: Say Hello to the Print Function

The first Python element that you need to learn is the **print** function. This command will give you the result of what you have programmed or the **output**. When you are programming, as you will see in a little bit, the print function will give you the values you requested. This means that the **parameters** that you have established will be shown. These parameters are used in what is called **syntax**. To make it easy for you to imagine, the syntax of the Python code is similar to a sentence structure. It will give the commands of what you want to see. Let's take a look at what these parameters are.

Parameters

All code languages have something that is called a **parameter**. These variables define what will be done in that specific syntax of the definition of the function (*Introduction to Python: Functions Cheatsheet*, n.d.). In python, these parameters are separated by a comma, which will establish what needs to be done. These elements will be placed inside a parenthesis, thus determining the syntax of the code.

When you build a syntax in python, some elements are mandatory. These are the object, separator (sep), end, file, and flush. If you were to place them within the code, it would look something like this:

Print(object, sep, end, file, flush)

Therefore, as you will see further along in this book, and with the examples I will provide, most of the code you develop in python will have this structure. For now, you don't have to worry about knowing what should be in each place because you will learn this in later chapters. What you need to know is that python has a structure—knowing this will make it easier for you to understand and identify the examples you see later on.

Let's look at the next important element of python: **variables**. You will give these names to each of the parts of your code that will hold a value or the reference to a value. This means that to place information in your code, you will need to establish the value for it. The information contained there will be used to generate your result. But let's not get ahead of ourselves. Continue on to the next section to learn more about Python variables and how to use them.

Variables

Variables are like containers that hold information or values in a program. We use variables in programming to store data that we want to use later. They allow us to name and use a piece of data throughout our program without remembering the value or type of data.

We use variables in programming to make our code more readable and easier to maintain. Instead of using the same value repeatedly, we can use a variable name that represents that value. If we need to change the value later, we only need to change it in one place instead of searching through our code for every instance of that value.

In python, variables are created by assigning a value to a name using the equal sign (=).

`x = 5`

Every time we use the variable "x" in our program, it will have a value of 5. Here are a few more examples:

`name = "Alice"`

For storing a string (text) in a variable named "name."

`age = 10`

For storing an integer (number) in a variable named "age."

`height = 1.5`

For storing a floating-point number (decimal) in a variable named "height."

`pi = 3.14`

For storing a constant value (pi) in a variable named "pi."

As you have just seen, variables can hold different data types, such as numbers, text, or other variables. When you want to assign a value to the memory of a Python program, you can use this basic element. This means that you can, for example, establish that:

```
name = "John Smith"
age = 37
weight = 140,5
```

The variable "name" has been given the value "John Smith," the variable "age" was assigned the value "37," and the variable "weight" was assigned the value "140,5." Therefore, when you ask the program to print the result or to give you the **output**, you will have to do the following:

```
print(name)
print(age)
print(weight)
```

And the **output** will be as follows:

John Smith

37

(140,5)

This means that your result will print exactly what you have asked it to according to the parameters established in your code. If you separate them in the print function with a comma, you will have all the answers in the same line. For example

```
print(name, age, weight)
```

The output will be

John Smith 37 (140, 5).

In python, we can use words and numbers, and, as you will see, these are **variable types** that will be described in the following chapters.

In the meantime, let me just say one last thing for variables: they can be substituted at any time during your code. As you program, unless you change the values attributed to each variable, they will remain the same. But you don't have to worry, these can be changed in a very easy way! For example, let's say that you want to change your age to 38, but you are already using 37 in another print function that is part of your code. You would need to just write a simple piece of code.

Simply take the previous code,

```
name = "John Smith"

age = 37

weight = 140,5
```

and write underneath it what you want to change it to,

```
name = "John Carrey"

age = 38

weight = 150,6
```

making it look like this:

```
name = "John Smith"

age = 37

weight = 140,5

name = "John Carrey"

age = 38

weight = 150,6
```

You can also group them to make it easier to see, name under the name, age under age, and weight under weight.

Now the output would be:

```
John Carrey

38

(150,6)
```

There you have it! Now you know how to declare a variable in your program and you also know how to change it. Simple, right? There should not be any error in the code you have just seen, and it should be easy to replicate with other examples on your computer. But variables have a few rules, which you need to know before you start using them.

Do's and Don'ts for Variables

When working with variables, there are a few rules you must consider. Here is a quick list for your reference:

Do These With Python

- When you name a variable, it must start with a letter (upper or lowercase) or the underscore sign (_). Attention! Hyphens (-) are not accepted.

Examples: Age, My_Age, my_name, _age, age5, and so on.

Pro tip: When you consider python and other languages, you must know that there are sets of conventions that programmers apply. These are not rules but rather best practices of the market to make the understanding of the code more universal. In python, this means not using camelCase, such as "MyFirstName," but rather my_first_name, with the words separated by the underscore (Tagliaferri, 2021). In addition to this, it is not common, or conventional, to see the first word capitalized when naming variables.

- Use meaningful names that show exactly what it is that the variable is storing.
- Use short words as possible.

Don'ts for Python Variables

- Don't start a variable with a number.

Example: 5_age, 9_name

- Don't use spaces in variable names.

- Don't use special characters.

- Don't use abbreviations that cannot be understood.

- Don't use reserved words as names for variables. Let's take a look at what these are.

Reserved Words

Reserved words in python, also known as **keywords**, are words used to express functions in the language. This means you cannot use them to identify variables because they will give the program the command to do something else. These words are usually used in the lower case form, except for the ones we will see in the table I will show you, and can sometimes vary according to the Python version you are using to program. For example, while Python 2 has 30 keywords, Python 3 added 3 more to the list, with a total of 33 (Lathkar, 2020). Remembering this list so that you don't use them to name your variables while coding is important. However, if you forget, there are two ways to find them.

The first is to prompt the program to list them for you by entering the following commands in the code interpreter (Lathkar, 2020):

```
>>> import keyword
>>> keyword.kwlist
```

You can also come back to the following list:

and	finally	None
as	false	not
assert	for	or
break	from	pass
class	global	raise
continue	if	return

def	import	True
del	in	try
elif	is	with
else	lambda	while
except	nonlocal	yield

Printing with F Literals

F-strings, also known as **formatted string literals**, are a way to use expressions inside string literals (Python, n.d.). These were introduced in Python 3.6 and provide a more concise and readable way to insert variables into string literals than traditional string formatting. Before this, the program had other ways of making strings that were considered more complicated and led the user to more errors (Jablonski, 2018). The "f" in the name of this function is for "fast."

Let's look at what this would look like when coding in python.

```
name = "Amanda"
age = 20
```

The traditional printing of this to identify the name and age would be:

```
print("Hi "+ name + " . Are you " + age + "?")
```

However, when using f-strings, this would be simpler by using the syntax:

```
print(f"Hi, {name}. Are you {age}?")
```

Here, you will see two differences from the regular print. The first is that, although we still use print(), the first character after you open the parenthesis will be the letter "f". Second, you don't need to use quotation marks or the "+" to join the sentences. All you need to do is place quotation marks at the beginning and the end of what you want to print and place the variables inside brackets ({ and }).

The output will be: Hi Amanda. Are you 20?

Although this might not seem like a huge time-saving improvement for this small code, if you consider those that contain more information, printing with f-strings will be an advantage. Furthermore, as you will see when you use this format with the variables between brackets, it will enable you to do other things with them, such as making all the letters capital or lowercase when you use the print function.

Although I am sure that you are doing great so far, sometimes, when we are learning, we may make mistakes. That is completely normal! There is no need to worry about that! When this happens, it means that your code has a bug and that you will need to carry out what is known as a debugging process. And, of course, I wouldn't be a good teacher if I did not show you how easy it is to fix them. Read on and see how to solve the problems you might encounter with your bug in just a few steps using IDLE.

Bugs and Debugging

The first thing you need to know is that if you find a bug, or an **exception**, in your code, you should not panic. Not at all. You should stop, take a breath, and try to see what you did wrong. Of course, when we have long lines of code, it might be hard to find exactly where the problem is. But, as you will see, you can use several software options and tricks to make this process easier.

What Is a Bug?

A bug in python appears when there is a mistake in your code. In other words, there can be an error in some part of your code that is disabling the IDLE from giving you the desired result. Suppose you are playing a game and you do not follow the instructions that come with it. This leads you to be unable to play the game correctly. In a situation where there is a bug in python, it means that the compiler cannot follow your instructions and because of this, the program cannot work.

There are three common types of bugs: logic, mathematical, or syntax (a-Rye, n.d.). When you have a **logic error,** there is a mistake in the reasoning you have used. Even if the code runs, it might not produce the expected result, which means there is probably an error somewhere down the line. This leads us to the second most common error: a **mathematical error**.

You have probably learned in school the acronym PEMDAS (parenthesis, exponent, divide, multiply, add, subtract) to determine the order you have to carry out math operations. If you haven't, PEMDAS is an easy way to remember the correct order of operations and the same logic works for python. If you are coding something and the mathematical answer is not what you expected, you need to check and see if you have written the code in this order. If it hasn't, you might want to rewrite or move around a few items to ensure the answer is what you expect.

The last most common type of problem is a **syntax error**. Remember when I told you that python has a syntax that needs to be followed so the program understands what you want? Well, if you don't follow the needed structure or leave something out, this will generate a syntax bug. Suppose you are just starting to program in python. In that case, this might be the most common mistake you identify in your code since it can take some time to adjust to all the specific terms and words that need to be used. But you will get there! To make it even easier to see where the mistake is located, read on to find out the methods you can use to debug your code.

What Is Debugging?

If finding an error in your Python program means you find a bug, it is only natural that when you want to fix it, the term used would be **debugging**. When you carry out this process, it means that you will fix the mistake that is halting the program from working. But you know what the best part is? Python has several debugging tools and software that you can use to help you find bugs—there is certainly no reason why you must find them by hand!

The first thing you need to know to make your debugging process easier is while you are building the code, you need to establish what is known as **breakpoints**. These are markers that you will place in the code to divide into parts, making your debug process easier. Imagine that instead of looking at several lines of code, you will only need to look at a section at a time—this is the advantage of adding breaks. And it is not hard at all!

To add a breakpoint to your code, all you need to do is enter the function **breakpoint()** at the bottom of the section of code you have written. Another way to do this is to right-click on the line where you want to add the breakpoint. Once you do this, a window will appear, and you can **set a breakpoint** or **clear breakpoint** in case you want to remove it. Here, you must know that when you add the breakpoint with the computer shortcut, the line where it was added will be highlighted in yellow, and this is only to indicate to the user where the break is located (Moura, 2021).

By adding breakpoints, you will be able to test sections between the breakpoints, making it easier to visualize where the error is. And if you are using IDLE to debug your code, this is even better. Yes, you read that right! You can debug your code with the IDLE application you downloaded when installing python. And this can be done with just a click of the button on the top toolbar where it says **Debug** and then **Debugger**. The debugger will open, and you should leave it like this and **run** your program.

If there are any problems in your code, they will appear in the debugging window. This is where you will see the main advantage of breaking the code into sections. The first thing you will notice is that the debugger will give you the **line number** where the mistake is—this information will be highlighted in blue. Having shorter lines of code makes it easier to identify in which line they are located. This line will also give you the error that the code presents.

In the debug window, you will see five options you can click on once the error is identified. They **go**, **step**, **over**, **out**, and **quit**. To run the full program line by line, you will click on "step," while if you want it to run until the next breakpoint, you must click on "go" (Moura, 2021). To end the execution, you will need to click on "quit," or you can just select the "out" button so that it moves to the next command. Finally, if you click on the "over" button, it will call off the function, and the debugger will not be used, moving on to the next section of the code.

While this is all good to know, we must remember that we are talking about the "print" function in this chapter. You might then be asking yourself why this debugging section is here. Here is some great news: You can also use the print function to debug your code. This is a much simpler way to check your code and see where the mistakes are. It might be even easier to debug the code with this function, so I have placed it here. Ready to take a look at how to do this?

Using the Print Function to Debug My Code

As I have mentioned, one of the awesome features of

the print function is that you can use it to debug your code. This means it will help you discover why your program is not working as expected. However, it is important to remark here that this function will only allow you to identify the behavior of a variable, for example, and not make a more complex analysis (Rudick, 2020). This means that if you are dealing with many lines of code, printing to debug can be something that will become a time-consuming and boring process since you will need to keep repeating it until you identify what is going on. Nevertheless, it is a useful function for simpler codes and identifying anything wrong with your logic.

Let's suppose we have the following:

age = 15

years = 5

yearsB = 3

And you want to make a sum of these two numbers to see what the individual's age will be in five years. In this case, we would use

print(age+years)

The output here should be 20; this is exactly the answer you will get if you print it. However, suppose that you have a long line of code where there are several variables, and you mistakenly write:

print(age+yearsB)

The result will come back with the answer 18. This is because you have added 15 (age) plus 3 (yearsB), thus resulting in the number you see. You will be able to identify the behavior and understand that there is a mistake because you know the final answer and the expected output was not it. Cool, right? Printing to debug is an easy and fast way to identify if there are any problems with what you have written.

Do's and Don'ts While Printing

To improve your experience with python, I have

22

provided a few tips about what you should or should not do when coding in python. Here are a few things you should consider:

Things to Do While Printing
- Use the print() function to output text to the console.

   Example: print("Hello, world!")

   Output: Hello, world!

- Use the "+" operator to concatenate strings when printing multiple values. We will see more about operators in the next chapter.

   Ex:

   name = "Carlos"

   age = 17

   print("My name is "+name+ " and I am " +str(age)+ " years old.")

   Output: My name is Carlos, and I am 17 years old.

   Observation: Here, you will note that I have left spaces between the words and the quotation marks. This is so the program will identify them and correctly space your phrase.

- Use formatted string literals (f-strings, which we will see briefly) to insert variables directly into a string.

   Example:

   name = "Carlos"

   age = 17

   print(f"My name is {name} and I am {age} years old.")

   Output: My name is Carlos, and I am 17 years old.

Things Not to Do While Printing
- Don't use multiple print() statements to output different lines of text. Apart from being inefficient, this makes the code harder to read.

Example:

name = "Carlos"

age = 17

print("My name is" + name)

print("My age is" + age)

Using Comments

Sometimes, when we are coding, we want to leave a type of "note" to others that might be reading the code. In this case, python has a commenting feature. Comments are used to add explanations or notes on the program's code, which help others understand your code. The syntax for using a comment on your code is the "#" symbol, followed by what you want to say. Anything that follows the hash symbol will be considered a comment, and the Python interpreter will not consider it part of the code.

These can be placed anywhere in the code as long as it does not interfere with your syntax. A few examples include:

#here are the parameters that should be used

name = "Amanda" #name will refer to the user name

age = 20 #age will be the user age

print(f"My name is {name} and I am {age} years old.")

#program should return and output with a user name and age in a sentence

Place all this information in your compiler. It will still only identify the name and the age since the rest of the text is preceded by the hash symbol. However, it is important to note that you should make your code as clean as possible to avoid using comments unless extremely necessary since they are considered to "pollute" the code and make it harder to read. As you read the next chapters, you will notice that on some occasions, I will use commenting within the code to make the examples clearer.

Escape Characters

Since Python has several rules, when one of them is broken, the result will appear in the output (Campbell, 2023). When you add a character to your syntax's sequence, you use an **escape character**. Usually, these exceptions are demonstrated using the \ (backslash) character. For example, suppose you want to print the following:

```
print(f'My name is "{name}" and I am "{age}" years old.")
```

Here, you added more double quotation marks inside the other ones, which is not allowed. Therefore, when you print, it will result in an error. To solve this problem, you would use the escape character, and it would look like this:

```
print(f'My name is \"{name}\" and I am \"{age}\" years old.")
```

Escape character	What it does
\n	Inserts a new line after or before a string
\\	Adds a backlash to the result that will be printed
\xhh	Here, you will need to add the "x" and the "hh" represents the hexadecimal number corresponding to a letter to obtain the result of letters and numbers. The sequence

	of numbers should be placed inside double quotation marks.
\ooo	The octal value is similar to the hexadecimal value but for octal numbers (sequences of three numbers). You will add the backlash and only the numbers; this syntax should be placed between single quotation marks.
\b	Adds a "backspace" to the code, such as removing spaces between texts that will be printed.
\f	Interpolates literal strings
\r	Creates raw strings, or pure strings
\'	Adds single quotation marks to the string you are creating (similar to the double quotes we saw in the example)
\t	Adds a space between the elements of the string

The output, in this case, would be:

My name is "Amanda," and I am "15" years old.

Additionally, a list of escape characters for Python (Campbell, 2023) makes it easy to remember and apply when giving special commands. Let's look at what they are :

Summary

In this chapter, you have learned the basic features of python: variables and the print function. I have shown you what variables are, how to name and use them, and how they are a part of all the code you will create. In addition, you have been introduced to the print function, which will always produce the result, or output, of your code. You also saw that you can use the print function to debug your code and find mistakes. Lastly, I have provided you with two tables: one with reserved words and one with escape characters. It will be essential to remember these as they play an important part when coding in python and will enable you to use the code more efficiently.

Assignments

Now that you know the use of variables and the print function, I propose a few exercises to practice what you have learned. The answers and the syntax that should have been used will be found at the end of this book.

Assignment 1: Print three sentences about yourself.

1. What is your name?

2. How old are you?

3. What is your favorite animal?

What to Do: Use the print() function to print three sentences about yourself. Refer to previous examples for help.

Assignment 2: Store your name, age, and favorite animal in a variable.

What to do: Use a variable to store your name, age, and favorite animal. Then, use an f-string and your variable to output the three sentences about yourself in your console window.

Assignment 3: Escape your sentences.

What to do: Separate every sentence about yourself

onto a new line using the escape character in Python.

Assignment 4: You recently had a change of heart and didn't like your current favorite animal, and you just had a birthday. Update your age and favorite animal.

What to do: Update your age variable and favorite animal variable to reflect the changes.

Challenge: Pyramids of Giza

Fun fact! Did you know about 2.3 million stone blocks were used to build one pyramid? Write a program to print out your Pyramid of Giza using everything you've learned about multi-line strings, f-strings, and variables.

It should look something like this:

```
                (0)
            (0)(0)(0)
        (0)(0)(0)(0)(0)
    (0)(0)(0)(0)(0)(0)(0)
```

Chapter 3: Python Data Types: Numbers and Operators

When you want to learn how to code, it is essential to understand what are known as **numeric types**. These variable types can hold number values and, like strings (which hold letter values), are a crucial building component in coding. They assist us in a variety of ways, including counting objects, doing math operations, keeping track of things, and much more.

As you progress through the chapters, knowing all the different number types, what you can do with them, and how to accomplish them will become increasingly crucial. In this chapter, we will look at the numeric types available in Python as well as the operations that can be used to perform mathematical functions. It will also be an opportunity to polish up your math skills, so if you need additional practice in this area, it will be great for you! Now, let's stop chatting and get this party started!

Numeric Types

In Python, there are three numeric types that you will be using. They are integers, floating-points (also known as "floats"), and complex numbers (Amos, 2020). Although it might seem like a complicated concept, it is rather simple. When you have **integers**, you can remember the word "integral," You will know that this variable only has whole numbers without decimal points. On the other hand, as you might deduce, **floats** are numbers with decimal points. Finally, **complex numbers** are those that have an imaginary part.

For example, 5, 10, and 15 will be considered integers, while 3.14 and 5.15 are floats. Complex numbers can be exemplified using the numbers and an arithmetic operator in the middle, such as 5+3x or 7+3y. A fun thing to know is that Python is one of the few languages that incorporate these imaginary numbers in its syntax, especially because it is so frequently used by scientific and computer graphic professionals that must deal with these situations. Remember when I told you NASA uses Python? Well, they certainly use these imaginary numbers for their calculations.

Therefore, when you perform calculations in Python, you can input any of these numerical characteristics you have seen. While this does not mean much on its own, after you have read the next section on operators, you will understand how they can be used and how useful they can be.

Operators

We will use an element called operators when talking about Python and mathematical functions. These symbols will be used to carry out calculations in your program and enable you to perform several other tasks. In Python, they are divided into arithmetic, comparison, and logical operators. When you apply each of these, they will tell your program what you want it to do with the variables you have listed in the compiler. Let's take a deeper look into each of the types of operators.

Arithmetic Operators

Arithmetic operators will allow the developer to perform mathematical operations with variables. They are divided into addition, subtraction, multiplication, division, floor division, modulo, and exponentiation (Amos, 2020). Do you want to see a few examples? Read on and look at what I will show you!

Let's say that we will use two different variables to demonstrate how to use these operators. They will be:

x = 5

y = 2

To **add** these numbers, we would use the following:

z = x+y

print(z)

Output: 7

To **subtract**, it would also be this simple:

z = x-y

```
print(z)
```

Output: 3

Here is an example of **multiplication**:

```
z = x*y
print(z)
```

Output: 10

And **division**:

```
z = x/y
print(z)
```

Output: 2.5

Here, in the division, I want to make a special remark. If you use Python 3, your division will always have a float value, even if the answer is an integral number, such as 6 divided by three equals 2. In this case, the output will be 2.0. If you want to perform integer division and get an integer result, you can use the floor division operator "//" as follows:

```
z = x//y
print(z)
```

Output: 3. As you can see, the number will be rounded up or down depending on the mathematical value of the decimal point.

The **modulo** operator (%) is used to get the remainder of a division operation. For example:

```
z = x%y
print(z)
```

Output: 5

Finally, we have the last operator, the **exponentiation**, where we use two (*) symbols. This function is used to raise a value to the power of the other, such as:

```
z = x**y
```

```
print(z)
```

Output: 10

These are all the arithmetic operators that can be used in Python. Simple, right? If you have been paying attention to your math class, you certainly will have no difficulty in remembering these, since the same symbols are used for the most part. However, as I mentioned, there are other operators that can be used when coding in Python, and we are going to see them right now.

Comparison Operators

Next, we have the comparison operators that, as the name suggests, will help you compare values in operations. To give you some examples, I will use the same numbers that we did before:

```
x = 5
y = 2
```

To see if these are **equal**, we would use the double equal sign (= =):

```
result = x = = y
print(result)
```

The output in this case would be False.

On the other hand, if we wanted to see if they are **different**, we would use the exclamation mark with the equal sign (!=):

```
result = x! = y
print(result)
```

In this case, the output would be True.

With comparison operators, we can also use the greater than or less then symbols to check if values are greater or less than others, in this case, it would look like this:

```
result = x>y
```

```
print(result)
```

For which the result would be True, since 5 is greater than 2, or we could have

```
result = x<y
```

```
print(result)
```

In which case the result would be False, since 5 is not less than 2.

In addition to this, you could also use the equal sign to transform the comparison into a **greater than or equal to** or a **less than or equal to** operation. In this case, the operators used would be the same, except with an equal (=) sign.

```
result = x> = y
```

```
print(result)
```

Output: True

```
result = x< = y
```

```
print(result)
```

Output: False

Logical Operators

Finally, we have the logic operators that will enable you to check if conditions are true or false by using specific signals. Let's take a look at some examples.

The first logical comparison operator we want to look at is **and** (and). This logical operator is used to check if both conditions are true. For example:

```
x = 5
```

```
y = 10
```

```
if x > 0 and y < 20:
```

```
print("Both conditions are True")
```

In this case, the output will be **Both conditions are True**.

Additionally, we can use the **or** operator (or) to check if at least one condition is true, such as

```
x = 5
y = 10
if x > 0 or y < 5:
print("At least one condition is True")
```

In this case, as you might imagine, the output will be **At least one condition is True**.

Finally, we have the last logical operator, **not** (not). In this case, the logical operator is used to reverse the logical state of the statement, usually used in **if statements**. If you don't know much about if statements, don't worry! We will also take a look at them later. Here, however, you must remember that the "not" operator can be used to identify the logic of an operation, such as:

```
x = true
if not x:
print("x is not True")
Else:
print("x is True")
```

In this case, the output will be **x is True** because we have established its characteristics in the beginning.

While all of these are exciting and important to learn, to use them adequately, there is one last necessary thing you must know or remember from what you have already learned in school. The acronym PEMDAS, or *Please Excuse My Dear Aunt Sally*, helps to remember the order in which operations are carried out. Just as you apply it in real-life mathematical operations, you will need to know this concept for programming and performing math operations in Python. Let's take a closer look.

Order of Operations (PEMDAS)

In Python, just like the math you learn in school, a specific order of operations needs to be followed when you consider multiple functions. This order is often referred to as PEMDAS, which stands for:

1. Parentheses
2. Exponents
3. Multiplication and Division (from left to right)
4. Addition and Subtraction (from left to right)

If you don't quite remember this from school or haven't learned this yet, let's look at some examples to see how this works in practice:

Example 1

x = 2 + 3 * 4

Here, we have addition (+) and multiplication (*) operators. According to PEMDAS, we need to perform the multiplication before the addition, so we first evaluate 3*4, which gives us 12. Then, we add 2 to 12, giving us a final result of 14. Therefore, x is equal to 14.

Example 2

y = (2 + 3) * 4

Here, we have parentheses (), addition (+), and multiplication (*) operators. According to PEMDAS, we need to perform the operation inside the parentheses before anything else, so we first evaluate 2+3, which gives us 5. Then, we multiply 5 by 4, giving us a final result of 20. Therefore, y is equal to 20.

Example 3

z = 8 / 4 * 2 ** 3 - 3

Here, we have division (/), multiplication (*), exponentiation (**), and subtraction (-) operators. According to PEMDAS, we need to perform the exponentiation first, so we evaluate 2**3, which gives us 8. Then, we need to address the multiplication and division operators from left to right. So, we must first perform the division 8/4, which gives us 2. Then, we perform the multiplication 2*8, which gives us 16. Finally, we subtract 3 from 16, giving us a final result of 13. Therefore, z is equal to 13.

As you can see, knowing how to apply PEMDAS will make it much easier for you to obtain the final result according to your expectation. You must consider this when you are programming to ensure that the final output is correct. If you find a different result manually, ensure that PEMDAS is correctly applied. Finally, I want to leave you once more with a reminder of how to easily remember the order of operations, which I learned a long time ago when I was in school. To remember PEMDAS, use the sentence *Please Excuse My Dear Aunt Sally*, where the first letter of each word refers to a letter in the concept, making it easier to remember!

Summary

This chapter was all about math! Yes, as you have seen, Python is excellent for making math calculations, and several operators enable you to do this. Do you remember what they are? You got it right! They are arithmetic, logical, and comparison operators. In addition, you have seen the importance of using PEMDAS in your operations and how to use them in Python. Now, to make sure you got everything straight, shall we try some exercises?

Assignments

Here are a few assignments that you should try in your compiler with coding to ensure you understand the concepts of numerical operators we have seen throughout this chapter.

Assignment 1: Numeric Types

Create a program that calculates the area of a square with a side length of 5. Assign the result to an area variable and print the area value to the console.

Assignment 2: Arithmetic Operators

Create a program that calculates the total price of 3 items that cost $10, $20, and $30, respectively, and adds 8% sales tax. Assign the result to a variable called total and print the total value to the console.

Assignment 3: Comparison Operators

Create a program that compares the age of two people, John and Jane. John is 25 years old, and Jane is 30 years old. Print True if John is younger than Jane; otherwise, print False.

Assignment 4: Logical Operators

Write a program that uses logical operators to determine if a number is between 5 and 10 (inclusive).

Assignment 5: Order of Operations

Write a program that calculates the value of 3 + 4 * 5 using the order of operations in Python.

Assignment 6: Combining Operators

Write a program that uses arithmetic and comparison operators to determine if the result of (5 + 7) * 2 is greater than or equal to 24.

Assignment 7: Using Parentheses

Write a program that uses parentheses to change the order of operations in the expression 10 / 5 * 2 and return the result.

Challenge: Solving an Equation

Solve the following equation using Python code and the order of operations (PEMDAS):

(12 / 3) * (8 + 2) - 4 ** 2

Hint: Remember that the order of operations (PEMDAS) is Parentheses, Exponents, Multiplication and Division (from left to right), and Addition and Subtraction (from left to right).

Chapter 4: Python Data Types: Strings and Other Data Types

In the last chapter, we learned about operators and how to apply them with numeric types. Did you know that some of them can also be used with strings? But you don't know what strings are? Don't worry, I will explain them to you in just a minute. In the meantime, you should know that this chapter will teach you about lists, tuples if statements, strings, and variables and how we can use them with different operators. Curious already? Well, then, let's move on and have a look at how!

Strings

In Python, a string is a sequence of characters. We use strings to store text and other types of data that consist of characters, such as letters, numbers, and symbols. In addition, you can recognize a string because it will be enclosed in single or double quotation marks (*Python Strings*, n.d.-b). We have, for example, "Hello, world!" or 'Hello, World!' as a pretty common string to print for developers who are beginning.

In this case, the string is enclosed in double quotes, and it contains the characters "H", "e", "l", "l", "o", ",", " ", "w", "o", "r", "l", "d", and "!" (*Python Strings*, n.d.-a). We can access individual characters in the string by their position (index) using square brackets:

```
first_letter = my_string[0]  # the first character of the string
print(first_letter)
Output: "H"
```

Here, you have seen that we added "0" between the brackets to ask for the first character. An important thing to know is that when you are looking for a specific position, you have to start the count from "0" and not from "1" to accurately find the position. Therefore, when you want to find specific information, remember to start counting from 0. But don't worry too much if you don't understand the concept; we will look at indexing lists and other specific information in this chapter.

In the meantime, did you know there is a way to combine two strings? Cool, right? This process is called **concatenation** and is done using the operator "+" within the code. Let's take a further look.

Concatenation

Remember when I gave you the first examples, way back in chapter 2 when we used this example:

name = "Amanda"

age = 20g

print("Hi "+ name + " . Are you " + age + "?")

And the final output was *Hi Amanda. Are you 20?*. Well, you didn't know it yet, but you were concatenating strings! This means you combine two or more strings by using the "+" operator in the print function. Let's take a look at another example:

greeting = "Hello"

name = "Alice"

message = greeting +", "+name +"!"

print(message)

```
greeting = "Hello"
name = "Alice"
message = greeting + ", " + name + "!"
print(message)
```

In this case, the output will be: Hello, Alice!. Here, we have established the first string by defining the first variable as "greeting" with the value of "Hello" and the second variable with the name "name" and the value "Alice." We have also established that the "message" variable will be the same as adding the greeting, plus a comma, plus the name, and finally, with the exclamation point. By doing this, you have created your string!

Santos Ozoemena

And you know what the best part is? You can create as many strings as you wish and add them to the print function. The possibilities are endless. How cool is it that you already know how to do this because of the previous exercises? Awesome, right? But you want to know what is even better? Read on to find out how you can **multiply** strings when using numbers.

Multiplying Strings

Sometimes, we want our program to repeat the same thing several times. However, instead of coding the program in a way that you need to repeat the same information, you can use string multiplication to achieve this task. How? Well, let's take a look at an example.

Suppose you want to print the "*" symbol five times. You don't need to type it in five times. All you need to do is write the following code:

```
stars = "*" * 5
```

```
print(stars)
```

And your output will be: *****.

How fun is that? Can you think about any other situation where you would need to print the same thing several times? How could this help you when programming?

The last two awesome features I want to show you regarding strings are simple. Although you might not constantly use them, they are cool features. These are the tools for transforming your string into all lowercase or all uppercase letters. This is done by using the **lower** or the **upper** functions. In the case of the code we already have, they would look like this:

```
my_greeting = "Hello, Alice!"
```

```
new_greeting = my_greeting.lower()
```

```
print(new_greeting)
```

The output will then be: hello, alice!

On the other hand, if you wanted to make them all uppercase, you would write the following code:

```
new_greeting = my_greeting.upper()
print(new_greeting)
```

The output will then be: HELLO, ALICE!

Cool, right?

Lists

The next thing you want to know is what a list is. Just as we have in our daily lives, a list is a collection of values. They can be composed of numbers or alphabetic characters. We use lists to store multiple values in a single variable. Let's look at a simple example of a list:

```
my_list = [1, 2, 3, 4, 5]
```

This list is composed of the numbers 1-5; as you can see, they are listed in between square brackets, which characterizes a list. In this case, your variable is named **my_list**, and the numbers within it are the values. As you saw in the strings section, we can access individual values in the list using square brackets and the index of the value if we start counting from 0. Let's look at another situation like this where we want to identify the second item of the list, or in this case, position 1:

```
second_value = my_list[1]
print(second_value)
```

Output: 2

In this case, we have created the variable **second_value**, and we requested that it identify the second position **[1]** from the list **my_list**. Once this was established, we requested that the program print the second_value variable, and the result was number 2, the second item on the list.

Another cool feature of lists is that we can **add** new values to them if needed by using the **append** function. In this case, to use the previous example, we have numbers 1-5, and want to add another number to it, let's say number 6. We would use the following:

41

```
my_list.append(6)
print(my_list)
Output: [1, 2, 3, 4, 5, 6]
```

Here, you have the previous **my_list** variable, and requested the **append** function to add the number 6 by adding the extension **.append** to the end of the variable. Next, when you requested it to print the new my_list, the result was a list from numbers 1 to 6.

You must be thinking that if you can add a number, you can also remove one, right? You are completely right! You can do that, indeed. This is done using the **remove** method, which will be added to the end of the my_list variable, just as you did with append. In this case, let's suppose you want to remove number 3 from the list you have created. The code would look like this:

```
my_list.remove(3)
print(my_list)
Output: [1, 2, 4, 5, 6]
```

As you can see, I have added the extension **.remove** to the end of the variable my_list and described the number **(3)**, which was the item I wanted to remove. When I requested that the compiler print the information, it gave me back the list 1-6 without the number 3. It is important to note that 6 appeared because we are writing the code sequentially without starting from scratch.

But what if you have a long list of numbers as a result? Do you know how you would count them? No! Not manually! There is a function in Python that will allow you to do this. It is the **len** function, short for **length**. Suppose this list is really long, and you want to check how many items are in it. In this case, we would not use the function by adding it to the end, but rather in a similar way to the print function. This is what it would look like for the same list of numbers we have been using:

```
list_length = len(my_list)
```

```
print(list_length)
```

Output: 5

As you can see, we created the new **list_length** variable and said that this variable equals the **len** of my_list, written in between parentheses. This means that printing the variable list_length will give us the number of items in the list. Here, you must note that the program considers that there are 5 numbers; thus, zero is not used in the calculation.

Ordering Lists

Sometimes you might have a list that you need to order. Suppose you have a list of random numbers that you want to be placed in numerical order. There is a function in Python that will enable you to do this, and it is called the **sort** function. Let's take a look at how this would work.

The following list has been defined with several numbers:

```
numbers = [3, 1, 4, 1, 5, 9, 2, 6, 5, 3, 5]
```

If we want to put this list in order from least to greatest, we can use the **sort()** function:

```
numbers.sort()
```

Now the list looks like this:

```
[1, 1, 2, 3, 3, 4, 5, 5, 5, 6, 9]
```

We can also order a list in reverse order, from greatest to least, by using the **reverse()** function:

```
numbers.reverse()
```

Now the list looks like this:

```
[9, 6, 5, 5, 5, 4, 3, 3, 2, 1, 1]
```

This can later be used with other lines of code to remove numbers, count the items in the list, and everything else you have already seen. But this is not all that lists can do. Remember when I told you we would take a deeper look into indexes? Well, now is the time to do it. Let's dive into indexes, lists, and strings and how they can relate to and be used within your

Python code.

Indexes

As you already know, we can use the **index()** function to find out exactly where in the list the number 5 is:

```
index = numbers.index(5)
```

```
print("The number 5 is at index", index, "in the list.")
```

If we have the list of numbers below:

```
numbers = [3, 1, 4, 1, 5, 9, 2, 6, 5, 3, 5]
```

The code will be:

```
index = numbers.index(5)
```

```
print("The number 5 is at index", index, "in the list.")
```

The output will be: The number 5 is at index 4 in the list. Remember that they start counting from 0, so when you count "as usual," the answer will be 5, but when you count with Python, the answer will be 4.

Lists, Strings, and Indexes

While most of the examples I have given so far used numbers, you can also use lists and indexes with strings. This is because this list of values in Python is like a bag filled with toys, where each toy will be called an **element**. The same things you can do with numbers, removing, adding, or changing, can be done with strings as well. Let's take a look at a few examples.

Let's say we have a list of toys:

```
toys = ["ball", "doll", "car", "puzzle"]
```

To access a specific element in the list, we use an index, right? So, to access the first element in our toy list (which is "ball"), we would use the index 0:

```
print(toys[0])
```

Output: ball

To access the third element in the list (which is "car"), we would use index 2:

```
print(toys[2])
```

Output: car

To change an element in a list with a string by using its index, you would type in the following code:

```
toys[1] = "teddy bear"
print(toys)
```

Output: ball, teddy bear, car, puzzle

And to add elements to the end of this list by using the append method, the code would look like this:

```
toys.append("train")
print(toys)
```

Output: ball, teddy bear, car, puzzle, train

As you can see, as long as the list is contained within the square brackets and separated by the comma (,), you can use indexes with them. But if you think that is all, you are in for a big surprise! We can do two more things with lists, whether they contain numbers or strings. These are: slicing and changing the list and its elements. Read on to find out how to do this!

Slicing and Lists

Slicing is a way to get a part of the list. It's like cutting a slice of cake from a whole cake. To slice a list, we use a colon (:). Let's suppose we have a list of fruits as follows:

```
fruits = ['apple', 'banana', 'cherry', 'date']
```

And that from this list, you want to select only items 1 (the second) and 3 (the fourth). You would write your code in the following manner:

```
print(fruits[1:3])
```

The output, in this case, would be: banana, date.

Quite simple, right? Suppose you want to hide the starting or ending index to slice from the beginning or up to the end of the list, respectively. This means that you would write your code like this:

```
fruits = ['apple', 'banana', 'cherry', 'date']
print(fruits[:2]) #Output: ['apple', 'banana']
print(fruits[2:]) #Output: ['cherry', 'date']
print(fruits[:]) #Output: ['apple', 'banana', 'cherry', 'date']
```

In these examples, fruits[:2] means getting a slice of the list of the fruits from the beginning up to (but not including) index 2, so it returns ['apple', 'banana']. In the second example, fruits[2:] means getting a slice of the list of fruits from index 2 up to the end, so it returns ['cherry', 'date']. Finally, fruits[:] means getting a slice of the list of the whole fruits, so it returns ['apple', 'banana', 'cherry', 'date'].

Mutable (Changeable) List

As you have also seen in some examples, a list in Python is mutable, enabling the developer to change the elements contained in it. Let's go back to our list of fruits, but now using only three elements:

```
fruits = ['apple', 'banana', 'orange']
```

You can modify the elements in the list like this:

```
fruits[0] = 'pear'
```

This will change the first element of the list to 'pear', and the output will be: pear, banana, or orange.

```
fruits = ['apple', 'banana', 'orange']

# Display the original list
print("Original list:", ', '.join(fruits))

# Mutation: Change the first element to 'pear'
fruits[0] = 'pear'

# Display the modified list
print("Modified list:", ', '.join(fruits))
```

Apart from this, you can also add elements to the list by

46

using **append**:

```
fruits.append('grape')
```

Which would make the output: pear, banana, orange, grape, adding 'grape' to the end of the list.

Now, suppose that you don't want to add the element to the end of the list but rather to the middle or in a certain position. You can also do this! Inserting an element at a specific position in the list would look like this:

```
fruits.insert(1, 'kiwi')
```

This will insert 'kiwi' at the second position in the list (remember that Python indexes start at 0). The output would then be pear, kiwi, banana, orange, and grape.

Next, you can also remove elements from the list by using this code:

```
fruits.remove('banana')
```

This will remove 'banana' from the list since the code will identify the specific characters of the word in the string. However, if you want to remove an element at a specific position, you can use the **del** statement:

```
del fruits[0]
```

Which will remove the first element of the list, making the output be: kiwi, banana, orange, and grape. Here, we deleted 'pear,' which was the first element.

Tuples

A tuple is similar to a list but has one major difference: it is immutable, meaning you cannot change its values once it is created (*Python Tuple (with Examples)*, n.d.). A tuple is created by enclosing values in parentheses and separating them with commas. Tuples are usually used when storing a collection of items that shouldn't be changed. Once you create a tuple, you can't add or remove items from it or change the values of the items in it.

For example, let's say we want to create a tuple to represent the x and y coordinates of a point:

point = (3, 5)

Once we create this tuple, we cannot change the values of 3 and 5. We can access the values of a tuple using indexing, just like with a list:

x = point[0] #x is now 3

y = point[1] #y is now 5

We can also use a tuple to return multiple values from a function:

def divide_numbers(a, b):

quotient = a // b

remainder = a % b

return quotient, remainder

result = divide_numbers(10, 3)

The result is now (3, 1)

```
def divide_numbers(a, b):
    quotient = a // b
    remainder = a % b
    return quotient, remainder

result = divide_numbers(10, 3)
print("The result is now", result)
```

We can also use the **divide_numbers** function to return a tuple containing the quotient and remainder of the division. We can then use indexing to access the individual values. Following the list that we had before, we would have the result:

quotient = result[0] # quotient is now 3

remainder = result[1] # remainder is now 1

Just as lists have their own functions, so do tuples. This means that you can **compare (CMP), convert a list into a tuple**

(seq), have the program return minimum and maximum values (min(tuple) and max(tuple)), and check the length of a tuple (len (tuple)) (*Python - Tuples*, 2019). In addition, you can use all of the other operators we have seen before with tuples: iterations, repetition, length, concatenation, and membership.

I bet you can see how tuples can be useful, but maybe there is still some doubt as to why we would use tuples instead of lists. If that is the case, don't worry. We will tackle these differences and the various applications in the following section of this book.

When to Use Tuples Over Lists

Tuples and lists are used to store collections of items in Python; you remember this, correct?. However, there are some differences between the two that make them better suited for different tasks. For example, if you wanted to store the (x,y) coordinates of a point on a graph, you could use a tuple, as we have seen in the previous section:

point = (3, 5)

This tuple has two values: 3 and 5. You can't add or remove values from the tuple or change the values of the existing items. However, you can access the individual items using their indexes:

x = point[0]

y = point[1]

Lists, however, are mutable, which means they can be changed. You can add or remove items from a list or change the values of the items in the list. This makes lists more flexible than tuples but also means that they are slightly slower and take up more memory.

So when should you use a tuple instead of a list? According to *Python Tuple (with Examples) (n.d.)*, you might use a tuple:

- When you want to protect the data in the list so that it is not changed or write-protected.

- When you want to store a collection of items that shouldn't be changed, like the (x,y) coordinates of a point or the RGB values of a color.
- When you have different data types, such as numbers and letters.
- When you want to store a collection of items that have a specific order but don't need to be changed. For example, the days of the week (Monday, Tuesday, Wednesday, etc.) could be stored in a tuple.
- When you want the program to respond faster.
- When you want to use a collection of items as a key in a dictionary. Tuples are immutable, so they can be used as keys, while lists can't.

Data Types In Python

When we consider variables in Python, we must know that they can store any data type. This means that they can store letters, numbers, or symbols. However, how each of these will be stored, and the "format" given to them will depend on the type of data you have. For a quick overview before we dive deeper, here is a small list of the data types available in Python (Sturtz, 2018):

- **Numbers**
  - **Integers:** These are whole numbers that can be positive, negative, or zero. For example, 1, -5, 0, 100.
  - **Floats:** These are numbers with a decimal point. They can also be positive, negative, or zero. For example, 3.14, -2.5, 0.0, 1.0.
  - **Complex numbers** are numbers associated with an imaginary variable, such as 2 +3y.
- **Strings** are a sequence of characters that can be letters, numbers, and symbols. They are used to represent text in programming. For example: "hello world", "12345", "!@#$%".

- **Booleans**: These are data types that can only be "True" or "False". They are often used in conditional statements to determine whether a certain condition is met.

We have already seen the first three types together with **complex numbers**, which leaves the **boolean** data type to learn. As you will see, these data types are really easy to understand since their output can only be one of two: True or False. They represent whether a statement or condition is true or false. Can you remember where you saw this before? You are correct if you say in the logical and comparison operators! This is exactly where you have seen them!

Let's remember one of the situations we have seen:

x = 5

y = 10

print(x < y) #This will print True because 5 is less than 10

print(x > y) #This will print False because 5 is not greater than 10

But you can also have something known as a **boolean variable**, where you establish if a determined variable is true or false. For example:

is_raining = True

is_sunny = False

print(is_raining) #This will print True

print(is_sunny) #This will print False

Finally, you can use boolean statements to make complex analyses of variables and situations. This will be done by using **boolean operators**: and, or, and not. Take a look below:

x = 5

y = 10

z = 15

print(x < y and y < z) #This will print "True" because both conditions are true

print(x < y and y > z) #This will print "False" because only the first condition is true

print(x > y or y < z) #This will print "True" because at least one of the conditions is true

print(not x < y) #This will print "False" because x < y is true, but not negated by the "not" operator.

Advanced-Data Types

Apart from the "basic" data types that we have seen in the previous section, Python also provides the user with what is known as **advanced data types**. These include four categories, of which we have already seen two: lists and tuples. In addition to these, we also have sets and dictionaries that we will talk about now and have a quick recap on the first two (*Python Data Types*, 2023).

- **Lists**: These are used for storing and manipulating multiple values in a single variable. You can use different operators and functions to manipulate lists in Python, such as + to concatenate two lists and append() to add an element to a list.
- **Tuples**: These data structures in Python allow you to store a collection of values. Unlike lists, tuples are immutable, meaning their contents cannot be changed once they are created.
- **Dictionaries**: These are used to store key-value pairs. You can use different functions to manipulate dictionaries in Python, such as keys() to get a list of keys and values() to get a list of values. Let's look at an example:

person = {"name": "John", "age": 30, "city": "New York"}

#get list of keys

```
print(person.keys())
```

The output, in this case, will be: name, age, city

```
#get list of values
print(person.values())
```

In this case, the output will be: John, 30, New York

- **Sets**: These are lists of items that are out of order and not necessarily of the same type. These items will be placed inside curly brackets ({ }) and are separated by a comma. One of the possibilities of using sets is that you can use the "|" operator to join two different types of sets, as you will see as follows:

```
my_set = {26, 8, 9, 7, "hello", 1, "bye"}
print(my_set)
```

The output, in this case, will be: bye, hello, 1, 7, 8, 9, 26.

If we had two sets, for example, we could also join them:

```
set_A = {"grape", "apple", "orange"}
set_B = {1, 3, 5, 7, 9}
print("My new set is = ", set_A | set_B)
```

The output, in this case, will be: My new set is = 1, 3, orange, 5, 7, 9, grape, apple.

Finally, the last thing you can do with sets is to compare if there are any similar elements between those that you want to analyze. Suppose that you have two sets:

```
fruits = {"apple", "orange", "bananas"}
ingredients = {"flour", "sugar", "apple", "butter"}
```

We would then ask the program to print where

there is an **intersection** between both lists.

```
print(fruits&ingredients)
```

In this case, the output will be Apple.

Converting Between Data Types

Like in many other programming languages, in Python, you can convert between different data types. This means that you will be using type conversion functions to make, for example, an integer into a string, a float into an integer, or a string into a float. In addition, you can also transform a list into a tuple or vice-versa and make changes in boolean functions. How? Well, here are some examples of how this can be done:

Converting a String to an Integer

To convert a string to an integer, you can use the int() function, such as:

```
my_string = "123"

my_int = int(my_string)

print(my_int) #Output: 123
```

Converting an Integer to a String

You can use the str() function to convert an integer to a string. For example:

```
my_int = 123

my_string = str(my_int)

print(my_string) #Output: "123"
```

Converting a String to a Float

You can use the float() function to convert a string to a float.

```
my_string = "3.14"

my_float = float(my_string)

print(my_float) #Output: 3.14
```

Converting a Float to an Integer

You can use the int() function to convert a float to an

integer. This will round down to the nearest integer:

```
my_float = 3.14
my_int = int(my_float)
print(my_int) #Output: 3
```

Converting a List to a Tuple
You can use the tuple() function to convert a list to a tuple.

```
my_list = [1, 2, 3]
my_tuple = tuple(my_list)
print(my_tuple) # Output: (1, 2, 3)
```

Converting a Tuple to a List
```
my_tuple = (1, 2, 3)
my_list = list(my_tuple)
print(my_list) # Output: [1, 2, 3]
```

In addition, in Python, the **bool()** function is used to convert a value to a boolean data type. As you already know, the boolean value can be either True or False. Here are some examples of all values that are considered **True**:

```
print(bool(10)) # Output: True
print(bool("hello")) # Output: True
print(bool([1, 2, 3])) # Output: True
```

There are also instances in which the result is False. These will generally happen when the value is zero or if there are empty data sets, such as empty strings (""), empty lists ([]), empty tuples (()), and empty dictionaries ({}) (*Python Booleans*, n.d.).

Working With User Input
Although we have seen many parts of how to code, sometimes, we need to consider that our program needs input from the user. This means, for example, that they will put their name in a specific field, and the program will return with a

personalized greeting using their name. In Python, this is totally possible! We can do this by using a function known as **input()**. Essentially, this means that you are telling the program to consider the information the user has added. Let's take a look at how this works.

Storing User Input in Variables

In the following example, we will store the input the user gives into the variable. The code would look something like this:

```
name = input("What is your name? ")
print("Hello, " + name + "!")
```

In this example, the input() function is used to get the user's name, and the print() function is used to print a greeting that includes the user's name. When you run this code, the program will wait for the user to enter some text and press the enter key. The text that the user enters will be stored in the name variable.

The output, in this case, will vary according to the name of each user, meaning that there could be several options, such as:

Hello, Alice!

Hello, John!

And so on.

Converting User Input to Other Data Types

However, sometimes we might need the user input to be transformed into different data types because we will use this information for other parts of the program. This could mean changing an **int** into a **float** or any other options you have previously seen. If this is the case, there is no problem! Python can do this as well.

You can convert the user's input to a different data type using type conversion functions. For example, if you want to get a number from the user, you can use the int() function to convert the input to an integer:

```
age = int(input("What is your age? "))
print("You will be " + str(age + 1) + " next year.")
```

In this illustration, we have asked the user to input his age and calculated how old they would be in the next year by adding one. In this case, if the user added to the program the input that they are 10, the output would be *You will be 11 next year.* Here, the input() function is used to get the user's age as a string, the int() function is used to convert it to an integer, and the print() function is used to print a message that includes the user's age plus one.

Pro tip: It's important to note that the input() function always returns a string, so if you want to use the user's input as a number or perform mathematical operations on it, you'll need to convert it to the appropriate data type first.

Summary

Wow! This chapter had a lot of information, right? I know! Did you manage to follow everything? I hope you did! Even if you didn't, you could go back to take a second look and practice with the examples to ensure you have understood the concepts. As you read, you learned all about Python data types and how to work with them. We saw examples of sets, dictionaries, boolean, and how to convert different data types into others. We also learned a really new cool feature, input, that will enable your program to interact with others. How awesome is that? To ensure you understand everything, here are a few exercises to try. If you have any doubts, don't be afraid to go back; as usual, the answers and explanations will be at the end of the book.

Assignments

1. Write a program that asks the user for their name and age, stores the values in variables, and then prints them out in a sentence.

2. Write a program that calculates the area of a rectangle using the length and width entered by the user. Print the result.

3. Write a program that converts degrees Celsius to degrees Fahrenheit. Ask the user for the temperature in Celsius and print the converted temperature.

4. Write a program that takes the user's birth year as input and calculates their age. Print the result.

5. Write a program that converts kilometers to miles. Ask the user for the distance in kilometers and print the converted distance.

6. Write a program that takes the user's name and favorite color as input and prints out a sentence that says "<name>'s favorite color is <color>."

7. Write a program that calculates the area of a triangle using the base and height entered by the user. Print the result.

Challenge:

Write a program that calculates the area and circumference of a circle using the radius entered by the user. Print the results.

Chapter 5: Python Loops

To understand what a loop is, I want to give you a simple example. Suppose you try logging into your video game or email with your username and password. It won't let you in until you get it right, correct? This means that you will be on the login screen until you have placed the proper username and password so you can get in. This is an example of a loop working. In a loop, your program keeps running the same information until a certain condition is met. In the case of your videogame or email, the screen will be the same until you get it correct, thus breaking the loop.

It is possible to do this in Python and make your program repeat the same thing until the condition is achieved. There are three main types of loops in Python, which we will see in this chapter. They are the **for loop**, **while loop**, and the **nested loops**. Let's look at each of these and how you can use them.

```
list of items to go through     number of times to repeat

start for loop

for planet in planets:
    print(f"We are now on {planet}!")

block of code to repeat
```

Before we start, I just want to warn you in this chapter that, we will see some Python statements using what is known as a **condition** using ifs, whiles, and other terms. If you don't quite understand them at first, don't worry. We are going to learn more about these in Chapter 7. The main thing here is that you understand how the loops work and the logic of how they can be applied. Once this is done, it will be a walk in the park to understand the rest.

Basic Loops

A for loop is used to repeat instructions for each item in a list or sequence. You already know that there are three types of loops, and I have given you an example of what loops do. As you will see in the following sections, most of the loops are used for the same reason, meaning they have similar functions. However, what will differ between them is how they are written or, in other words, their syntax. Something else that will change is how long it will take each of them to run, depending on what you are asking it to do. Here are the basic forms of loops in Python and their explanations.

For Loops

The first type of loop I want to talk to you about is the **for loop**. This kind of loop is a way to repeat a set of instructions for each item in a list or sequence. Think of it like a machine that goes through each item in a list and does something with it, one at a time. This type of loop is faster since it will execute several statements as many times as needed while making the code shorter.

According to *Looping in Python (For, While, Nested Loops)* 2023), these loops work well with strings, lists, and tuples, and the condition will be **True** until all the variables are accessed. An example of the for loop syntax is:

For (value) in (n):

```
# Printing numbers from 1 to 5
for i in range(1, 6):
    print(i)
```

After which, you will add the code block.

Suppose you want to create a list where your program will state all the numbers up to 5. This means that the "final limit" is 5, and it should keep counting until it reaches this number. The code for this would look as follows:

x = 5

For y in range(0, x): #This means that we want to find y in the range from 0 to 5, which are all the numbers within this range.

print(y) #remember to indent the statement so that there is no problem with your code

The output, in this case, will be:

0

1

2

3

4

Here, there are a couple of things you must consider. The first is not to forget the colon (:) after the for statement. The other is that you must indent the print function within the code so it can recognize the information. Let's look at another example:

Suppose that we have a list of fruits as follows,

fruits = "oranges", "apples", "bananas", "lemons"

And we want the list to stop once we have reached bananas. We can use a for loop for this. The syntax would look like this:

```
fruits = "oranges", "apples", "bananas", "lemons"
For fruit in fruits:
    print(fruit)
    if fruit = = "bananas":
        print("We've reached bananas")
        break #add a keyword to exit the loop once the condition is reached
```

The output, in this case, will be "We've reached bananas".

In this code, we are first defining the list of fruits. Then, we use a **for loop** to iterate over each list element. Inside the loop, we print the current fruit being processed. We then check if the current fruit is equal to "bananas" using an if statement. If it is, we print a message to indicate that we've reached bananas and then use the break keyword to exit the loop.

An example of the for loop is the password situation I described before. In this case, you will input the information until the correct password is inserted. When this happens, the loop will stop running, and you will be taken to the next screen because the condition has been met.

You can use this feature with as many examples and data types as you wish ce the for loop is rea, But this is not the only type of loop you can have in Python. Let's look at the next loop we can use in Python, the white loop.

While Loop

The **while loop** will allow you to repeat a set of instructions as long as a certain condition is true. This means the program will continue running until the condition is no longer met. For example, you can request that the program keeps counting until it reaches a number greater than or equal to 10. In this case, once the count reaches this number, the condition will no longer be **true**, thus interrupting the loop.

```python
# Printing numbers from 1 to 5 using a while loop
count = 1
while count <= 5:
    print(count)
    count += 1
```

Let's take a look at an example:

count = 0

while count < = 10:

    print(count)

    count + = 1

In this case, the output will be

0

1

2

3

4

5

6

7

8

9

10

Because we have reached the condition where the last number is **less than or equal to** 10. In this example, the loop repeats the instruction to print the current value of the count as long as the count is less than or equal to 10. It prints "0", then "1", then "2", then "3", and so on. In this syntax, a condition is a statement that is either **true** or **false**. The code inside the loop will be executed as long as the condition is true.

As you have seen, we used the syntax

while (expression): #Here, the expression will be what you want the program to do, such as "count" in our example. Don't forget the colon!

Statement (s) #Here is the statement or the line of code that will establish the condition you want the program to perform.

There is one last type of loop that we are going to see, and this is called the nested loop.

Nested Loop

The **nested loop**, as the name might suggest: Enables you to use two or more for or while loops within others. This makes it easy to establish several conditions within your code to solve one or more issues you might have.

```
# Printing a 3×3 grid using nested loops
for i in range(3):
    for j in range(3):
        print(i, j)
```

Output:

```
0 0
0 1
0 2
1 0
1 1
1 2
2 0
2 1
2 2
```

In this case, the syntax could be like this:

for in x: #establishing the for loop

(add the code here)

while in x: #establishing the while loop with the for loop

(add the code here)

Let's look at what an example would look like.

Here we want to create a loop that will go over the numbers 0-9. Therefore, we will establish a range:

for x in range(3): #Loop over the numbers 0 to 3

for y in range(3): #Loop over the numbers 0 to 3

print(x * y, end = " ") # Print the product of x and y

In this case, your output will be a series of numbers that are: 0 0 0 0 1 2 0 2 4 because you have established that you want the program to count a range of the first three numbers (0-2) and then multiply each number to achieve the result.

This code uses two **loops**, one inside the other, as you can see by the indentation added to the code. In this case, the indentation will determine that one of the for loops is inside the other. While the outer loop iterates over the numbers 0 to 3, the inner loop also iterates over the numbers 0 to 3. Inside the inner loop, we multiply x and y and print the result. We use the end parameter to tell Python to separate the printed values with a space instead of a newline character.

How To Build Loops

Now that you have seen the basic information about loops, we can dive deeper to understand some of their specific components. In this section, we will look at loop control statements and a few other functions in Python with loops.

Loop Control Statements

First, you should know that loops have something called **control statements**. You might remember these keywords from the reserved words we saw in chapter two. These will instruct the program to stop the loop and move on to the next section once the condition has been fulfilled. In Python, there are three specific keywords to do this. They are:

- **Break**: Adding the keyword "break" to the end of the loop will stop the processing and move on to the next part of the code, just as we saw in the first example with loops I gave you. Here, the control of the program will be transferred to the statement after the keyword.
- **Continue**: Adding the keyword "continue" will cause the statement next to the word not to be processed after the loop conditions are fulfilled. When you have the continue keyword, the code will stop running after the loop condition is achieved.
- **Pass**: Adding the keyword "pass," will cause the program to "skip" the loop. It is used when the loop is necessary for the program to make sense (or for its development), but it does not need to be executed.

Iterating Loops With Range Functions

Remember that we saw in one of the exercises that we wanted a **range** of numbers within a list? This type of function is called a **range function**; you can create (iterate) loops to use these. Let's use the statement we used before so you can have a better visualization:

```
for num in range(0, 6):
```

```
print(num)
```

This means I have requested the program to print a range of numbers starting from 0 and going up to 6 and, therefore, my output will be:

0

1

2

3

4

5

If, on the other hand, I had stated in the code that I wanted:

```
for num in range(1, 6):
```

```
print(num)
```

The output would not start from 0 but rather from 1 since I have stated that the first number I want to be considered is 1. The syntax of the functions, in these cases, is:

```
range(start, stop, step)
```

In this syntax, the start is the first number in the sequence, the stop is the last number (which is not included), and the step is the amount the sequence increases each time (1 by default).

Loops Using Lists

Did you know that you can use loops with lists and not only with single data types? How cool is that? Well, right now, I will show you how these can be used so you can start applying them to your development process.

Suppose we have a list of your favorite colors:

```
colors = ["red", "blue", "green", "yellow"]
```

You can use a **for loop** in Python to go through each color in the list and do something with it, like this:

```
colors = ["red", "blue", "green", "yellow"]
for color in colors:
    print("My favorite color is " + color)
```

When you apply this condition to the code, you want to select a color in the colors list. With the code you have seen above, it will print "My favorite color is red," then "My favorite color is blue," then "My favorite color is green," and finally, "My favorite color is yellow."

Summary

In this chapter, you have learned everything about loops in Python and how they can be used in your development process to ensure that certain conditions are met. You have seen that Python has three main types of loops: for, while, and nested, and that these can be used with several data types. You can now write a program with these characteristics; how fun is that? To ensure you understand these concepts, here are a few exercises to practice.

Assignments

1. Write a program using a for loop to print all the even numbers between 1 and 20.

   Expected output: 2 4 6 8 10 12 14 16 18 20

2. Write a program using a while loop to find the sum of all the numbers between 1 and 100.

   Expected output: 5050

3. Write a program using a for loop to print the

multiplication table for the number 5.

Expected output:

5 x 1 = 5

5 x 2 = 10

5 x 3 = 15

5 x 4 = 20

5 x 5 = 25

5 x 6 = 30

5 x 7 = 35

5 x 8 = 40

5 x 9 = 45

5   x 10 = 50

1. Write a program using a while loop to print the Fibonacci sequence up to the 50th term.

   Expected output: 0 1 1 2 3 5 8 13 21 34

2. Write a program using a for loop to calculate the sum of all the multiples of 3 between 1 and 100.

   Expected output: 1683

3. Write a program using a while loop to print the first 10 prime numbers.

   Expected output: 2 3 5 7 11 13 17 19 23 29

Challenge

Create a program that asks the user to input a positive integer and then prints out the following pattern of asterisks (*) using a loop:

```
*
**
***
****
*****
```

The number of rows of asterisks should be equal to the input integer. For example, if the user inputs 5, the program should output the above pattern with 5 rows of asterisks.

Chapter 6: Turtles Are Fast! Introducing the Turtle Module

When developing a program in Python, you must know a concept known as a **module**. In programming, a module is a file that contains Python code that you can use in your own program—something like the blueprint you will use to build something with. Think of it like a treasure chest full of tools you can use to create something amazing! Each tool (or function) in the module is designed to do a specific job, just like a wrench is designed to turn bolts or a screwdriver designed to turn screws.

For example, if you want to make a program that can do some math calculations, you can use the math module. The math module has different functions that can help you add, subtract, multiply, or divide numbers. Or, if you want to make a program that can draw graphics, you can use the turtle module. The turtle module has functions that can draw shapes, lines, and even animations!

One great thing about Python modules is that you don't have to create all the code yourself. You can use modules that others have already created and shared with the world. This saves you a lot of time and effort and helps you learn from other people's code.

To use a module in your own program, the first thing you should do is **import** it. This means you tell Python to look in the module for the functions you want to use. Once you've imported the module, you can use its functions just like any other function in Python. Let's take a look at more information about modules.

Introduction to Modules

As I said before, a module is a Python file containing code that can be imported and used in other Python programs. Modules are useful for organizing code into reusable units and sharing code with other programmers. You might be asking yourself how you can use this amazing feature? *How do I import a Python module?* Well, there is no need to worry. I will teach you all about it now.

To use a module in a Python program, you first need to import it using the import statement. Here's an example:

```
import random
print(random.randint(1, 10))
```

In this example, the random module is imported by using the import statement, which is just another way of saying that you place the word **import** in front of the module you want to use. In this case, the random module provides functions for generating random numbers, among other things.

In the example above, the print() function will output a random integer between 1 and 10 using the **randint()** function from the random module. The randint() function takes two arguments, the lower and upper bounds of the range from which the random number should be selected.

But it gets even better! Did you know that you can also import specific functions or variables from a module using the keyword? For example:

```
from math import pi
print(pi)
```

In this example, the pi variable is imported from the math module using the **from** keyword. Therefore, for these cases, you would need to determine **from** where you want to import and **what** you want to import to use in your code. In this case, the pi variable contains the value of pi (approximately 3.14159) and can be used in the program without having to prefix it with the module's name.

But there is, even more you should know! Modules can also contain functions that you define yourself. To use a function from a module you have defined, you simply need to import the module as described above.

You first define the module the way you want to:

```
def greet(name): #define the code for mymodule.py
    print("Hello, " + name + "!")
```

Next, you will use the name you defined for your module, in this case, **mymodule**, to **import** it.

```
main.py
import mymodule
mymodule.greet("Alice")
```

In this example, a module called **mymodule** is defined in a separate file called **mymodule.py**. The module contains a function called **greet()** that takes a name argument and outputs a greeting message. In the main program (**main.py**), the **mymodule** module is imported using the import statement, and the greet() function is called with the argument "Alice". The program then outputs the message "Hello, Alice!".

You might be asking yourself where you can access all this information. Some Python libraries come with the program when you install it on your computer. These are usually installed in a folder in your computer called the /lib/site-packages (Dharmkar, n.d.). As you will notice, the end of a module will generally have the extension .py, making it easy to identify among the several other documents you will have on your computer. To find them, you must look into your computer's directory. In the official Python documentation, you can find a list of all the modules available in version 3 (*Python Module Index — Python 3.10.7 Documentation*, n.d.).

But why is this important? Well, the first reason is that you will be able to code easier once you learn how to use, import, and apply modules. The other is that I want to present you with one of the coolest Python modules: the Turtle Module!

What Is the Turtle Module?

The Turtle module is a built-in (which means it comes with the package) module in Python that allows users to create graphics and shapes by drawing lines and shapes using a virtual turtle. This module is often used in introductory programming courses to teach basic programming concepts. Now, can you imagine why apart from all the modules in Python, this is the one I picked to present to you? You are correct if you think it is because you can create graphics for your own game! With the Turtle module, you will be able to draw characters, for example, and design your own video game so you and your friends can play!

With this module, you can enhance your knowledge of how to program with Python. It will allow you to create amazing graphics, just like an artist would use a paintbrush to create a masterpiece. With the Turtle module, you can use simple commands to draw lines, shapes and even make your own animations! You can draw squares, circles, spirals, and even more complex shapes like flowers and animals. And once you've created your design, you can save it and share it with anyone!

One of the nice things you will notice is that you will use a turtle to draw on the screen. The turtle is like a digital pen that you can move around and tell it what to draw. You can use commands like "forward" to move the turtle in a straight line, "left" or "right" to turn the turtle, and "penup" and "pendown" to control when the turtle draws or not.

So, without further delay, let's look at how to use this tool and get this party started!

Importing the Turtle Module
The first thing you will need to do is to **import** the Turtle module. As you have seen, it will be named **turtle.py** in the list. The import process is as simple as you might imagine. All you have to do is type in the following code:

```
import turtle
```

And... that's it! Yes! You got that right! There is nothing else to do since the module is now downloaded, and you can start to use it. The next thing you will need to do is create a turtle. Let's see how to do this.

Creating a Turtle

Since the turtle is all about graphics, you must open a separate screen to draw the images you want. This is going to be done by creating a **variable** for it using the following code (Silaparasetty, 2020):

```
s = turtle.getscreen()
```

Once you do this, you will see that a new blank window (also called the screen) will open, and there will be a black triangle in the middle. Can you guess what it is? If you thought, *It was the turtle*, you are correct! This triangle is the turtle that you will use to give commands to. However, as with anything you have seen so far in Python, you will also need to create a **variable** to refer to the turtle to identify **what** exactly is going to receive your command. In this case, Silaparasetty (2020) suggests using the variable "t" so that you can remember that it is a "t" for "turtle," but the name I will leave up to you. Just remember that it needs to be an easy name that you will remember and that you can easily write because your code might get long. In this case, the code we are using would be:

```
t = turtle.Turtle()
```

Now, what you need to know is that you will be giving commands to the turtle by using "left," "right," "up," "down," and several others. The official Python documentation (Turtle — Turtle Graphics — Python 3.7.4 Documentation, 2019) lists all the commands you can use. I suggest you take a look before using the module and keep the link on hand in case you need to check any information.

So that you can see how easy it is to use the turtle module, let's take a look at an example of how to draw a square:

```
import turtle

my_turtle = turtle.Turtle() #Create a turtle object

# Move the turtle forward and turn it right four times to draw a square
```

```
for i in range(4):
    my_turtle.forward(100)
    my_turtle.right(90)
# Close the turtle window when finished
turtle.done()
```

What do you think? Simple, right?

Changing Background Colors, Filing Shapes With Color

Like I said before, the Python turtle module has several different commands you can use to change colors, draw shapes, and make graphics in general. Although there is a list you can use in the Python documentation, I wanted to show you how to use some of these commands with code examples. In all the examples I will show you, you will see the full syntax that needs to be used. However, you don't need to import the turtle code every time you use it if it has already been done. Here are the examples for you to use and test in your Python turtle screen.

1. **shape()**: This function is used to change the shape of the turtle cursor. The cursor can be changed to different shapes such as 'turtle', 'arrow', 'circle', etc.

    Syntax: turtle.shape(shape_name)
    Example:
    ```
    import turtle
    # Create a turtle object
    my_turtle = turtle.Turtle()
    # Set the turtle shape to 'turtle'
    my_turtle.shape('turtle')
    turtle.done()
    ```

2. **setup()**: This function is used to set up the dimensions of the turtle window.

Syntax: turtle.setup(width, height, startx, starty)

Example:

import turtle

Set up the turtle window with width = 500, height = 500

turtle.setup(500, 500)

turtle.done()

3. **bgcolor():** This function is used to set the background color of the turtle window.

Syntax: turtle.bgcolor(color)

Example:

import turtle

turtle.bgcolor('blue') #Set the background color of the turtle window to blue

turtle.done()

4. **screen():** This function is used to get the turtle window screen.

Syntax: turtle.Screen()

Example:

import turtle

screen = turtle.Screen() #Get the turtle window screen

turtle.done()

5. **colormode():** This function is used to set the color mode to 1.0 or 255.

Syntax: turtle.colormode(mode)

Example:

```
import turtle
turtle.colormode(255) #Set the color mode to 255
turtle.done()
```

6. **color()**: This function is used to set the pen color.

   Syntax: turtle.color(color)

   Example:
   ```
   import turtle
   turtle.color('red') #Set the pen color to red
   turtle.done()
   ```

7. **turtlesize()**: This function is used to set the size of the turtle cursor.

   Syntax: turtle.turtlesize(size_x, size_y, outline)

   Example:
   ```
   import turtle
   turtle.turtlesize(2, 2) #Set the size of the turtle
   ```
   cursor to 2x2
   ```
   turtle.done()
   ```

8. **resizemode()**: This function is used to set the resize mode of the turtle cursor.

   Syntax: turtle.resizemode(mode)

   Example:
   ```
   import turtle
   turtle.resizemode('user') #Set the resize mode of
   ```
   the turtle cursor to 'user'
   ```
   turtle.done()
   ```

9. **forward()**: This function is used to move the turtle cursor forward.

Syntax: turtle.forward(distance)

Example:

import turtle

my_turtle = turtle.Turtle() #Create a turtle object

my_turtle.forward(10) #Move the turtle forward by 10 units

turtle.done()

10. **back():** This function is used to move the turtle cursor backward.

Syntax: turtle.back(distance)

Example:

import turtle

my_turtle = turtle.Turtle()

my_turtle.back(100) #Move the turtle backward by 100 units

turtle.done()

11. **left():** This function is used to turn the turtle cursor left.

Syntax: turtle.left(angle)

Example:

import turtle

my_turtle = turtle.Turtle()

my_turtle.left(90) #Turn the turtle left by 90 degrees

turtle.done()

12. **right():** This function is used to turn the turtle cursor right.

Syntax: turtle.right(angle)

Example:

```
import turtle
my_turtle = turtle.Turtle()
my_turtle.right(90)
turtle.done()
```

13. pensize(): This function is used to set the thickness of the pen.

Syntax: turtle.pensize(size)

Example:

```
import turtle
my_turtle = turtle.Turtle()
my_turtle.pensize(5) #Set the thickness of the pen to 5
turtle.done()
```

14. fillcolor(): This function is used to set the fill color.

Syntax: turtle.fillcolor(color)

Example:

```
import turtle
my_turtle = turtle.Turtle()
my_turtle.fillcolor('blue') #Set the fill color to blue
turtle.done()
```

15. begin_fill(): This function is used to start filling a closed shape with the set fill color.

Syntax: turtle.begin_fill()

Example:

```
import turtle
```

```
my_turtle = turtle.Turtle()
my_turtle.fillcolor('blue') #Set the fill color to blue and start filling
my_turtle.begin_fill()
for i in range(4): #Draw a square
    my_turtle.forward(100)
    my_turtle.left(90)
# End the fill
my_turtle.end_fill()
turtle.done()
```

16. end_fill(): This function is used to end the fill started by begin_fill().

Syntax: turtle.end_fill()

Example:

```
import turtle
my_turtle = turtle.Turtle()
my_turtle.fillcolor('blue') #Set the fill color to blue and start filling
my_turtle.begin_fill()
for i in range(4): #Draw a square
    my_turtle.forward(100)
    my_turtle.left(90)
# End the fill
my_turtle.end_fill()
turtle.done()
```

17. circle(): This function is used to draw a circle.

Syntax: turtle.circle(radius, extent = None, steps =

None)

Example:

```
import turtle
my_turtle = turtle.Turtle()
my_turtle.circle(50) #Draw a circle with radius 50
turtle.done()
```

18. **stamp():** This function is used to stamp an image of the turtle cursor at the current position.

Syntax: turtle.stamp()

Example:

```
import turtle
my_turtle = turtle.Turtle()
for i in range(4): #Draw a square and stamp at
each corner
    my_turtle.forward(100)
    my_turtle.left(90)
    my_turtle.stamp()
turtle.done()
```

19. **penup():** This function is used to lift the pen up, so that it no longer draws when the turtle moves.

Syntax: turtle.penup()

Example:

```
import turtle
my_turtle = turtle.Turtle()
my_turtle.penup() #Lift the pen up and move to
a new position
my_turtle.goto(100, 100)
```

```
        my_turtle.pendown() #Put the pen down and
draw a square
        for i in range(4):
            my_turtle.forward(100)
            my_turtle.left(90)
        turtle.done()
```

20. write(): This function is used to write text at the current position of the turtle.

Syntax: turtle.write(s, move = False, align = "left", font = ("Arial", 8, "normal"))

Example:

```
import turtle
my_turtle = turtle.Turtle()
# Write some text at the current position
        my_turtle.write("Hello, world!", align = "center", font = ("Arial", 16, "normal"))
turtle.done()
```

In this example, the text "Hello, world!" is written in the turtle's current position. By giving it the commands, we have established that the "align" parameter is used to center the text horizontally, and the "font" parameter is used to set the font to Arial, size 16, and normal weight. By default, the turtle will not move after writing the text, but you can set the move parameter to **True** if you want it to move to a new position after writing. You can also change the different types of fonts and alignments according to your needs. Now that you know the basics it is up to you and your imagination to create new and awesome things!

Introduction to Hexadecimal System

One last thing I want to present to you in this chapter is something that will help you save your computer memory when you are coding: the hexadecimal system. As you might have studied in school, in our daily we use the decimal system— starting from number 1 to as much as you can count up to, each adding a digit when you reach the tens, hundreds, thousands, etc. As you might imagine, if you want to write a number that is too long, this could use a lot of space in your memory, especially if you are using it repeatedly.

Because of this limitation in coding programs, many systems use what is known as the **hexadecimal system** since it uses less memory to store the same information. This is a matter of your computer (bytes and bits will be used), but the point is that you can use this system as an alternative to coding when you want to save space since Python easily recognizes its elements.

To make it easy to understand, the first thing you should know is that the hexadecimal uses a base of 16. This means that it uses numbers 0-9 to represent specific values and the letters A to F to represent the numbers that range from 10 to 16. Think about it this way: Remember in school when you had to learn the Roman numerals and how each letter meant something different to make a number or a date? With the hexadecimal system, it is the same thing! Here, you will use a combination of numbers and letters to get the information you want.

Do you ever remember seeing a color system in which the color is referred to with a mixture of letters and numbers? In this case, we could say that we want our program to color the circle we have drawn with the color #FF0000 or, in other words, in red. This system is common for programming, and there are even tables that will give you the reference number for each color, such as #FFFF00 for yellow and #0000FF for blue.

In Python, we can represent hexadecimal values by prefixing them with "0x" or "0X". This means that before writing a hexadecimal number in your program, you must add these letters so the computer can understand what you want to say. For example, 0x2F represents the hexadecimal value 2F, equal to 47 in the decimal system. Let's see an example to make the explanation more clear. We will see how to transform hexadecimal numbers into decimal numbers.

The first thing we will do is to define some variables with hexadecimal values. We use the **hex()** function to convert these values to their hexadecimal representation and print them.

```
a = 0x2F

b = 0xABCD

c = 0xFFF
```

Here, we have defined the variables a, b, and c with different hexadecimal characteristics.

Next, we are going to use a formula to convert these hexadecimal numbers into decimal numbers so we can identify what they are:

```
d = int("2F", 16)

e = int("ABCD", 16)

f = int("FFF", 16)
```

After this is done, we will request the system to print the result. The code would look like this:

```
print(d)    # output: 47

print(e)    # output: 43981

print(f)    # output: 4095
```

Here, it is important to note that we can also convert hexadecimal values to decimal values using the int() function with the second argument set to 16. In this way, we can use hexadecimal values in our programs, especially when working with colors or other applications that use this system.

Summary

How fun was this chapter? With what you saw here, you can design your graphics and maybe code your video game. Now that has to be exciting, right? I have given you a few commands you can use with the **Turtle** module in Python, one of the most important modules for those who want to develop. Furthermore, you have also seen that Python has several other modules which will enable you to do almost anything by using blueprints previously provided by others. Don't forget that you can always check the official Python documentation online to obtain a complete list of these items.

You have also been introduced to the hexadecimal system, a concept that will help you save memory in your computer and allow your program to run faster. Remember that this type of coding is commonly used for working with web applications, so it is important to understand how it works just in case you need it. Let's go to our usual assignments and see if you remember what you have learned.

Assignments

1. Draw a square using Turtle.

2. Draw a triangle using Turtle and fill it with a color.

3. Draw a circle using Turtle.

4. Draw a star using Turtle.

5. Draw a spiral using Turtle.

6. Draw a snowflake using Turtle.

Challenge:

Draw a random walk using Turtle.

Chapter 7: Control Flow Statements: If, Else, Elif Statements

Control flow statements are instructions that tell a program which blocks of code to execute based on certain conditions. Remember when we discussed conditional statements? Well, this is where you would use them. Think about it as a logical process you want your program to follow while coding. For example, you might use control flow statements if you were designing a video game so that if character number 1 crosses the finish line first, they will be declared the winner; if not, then the program should give the position in which it arrived.

Therefore, you must consider that in programming, control flow statements are like the instructions you give someone to complete a task. For example, if you want someone to bake a cake, you might tell them to preheat the oven, mix the ingredients, and bake for a certain amount of time. Similarly, in Python, we use control flow statements to tell the computer what to do based on certain conditions. In Python, there are three conditional flow statements: those using **it**, others using **else**, and finally, a combination of both, the **elif**.

The most common control flow statement in Python is the **if** statement. An "if" statement is like a fork in the road—if a condition is met, the computer will go down one path. Otherwise, it will go down another. For example, if it's raining outside, you might want to bring an umbrella. In Python, you could use an "if" statement to tell the computer to print "Bring an umbrella" if it's raining outside.

Next, we have the **else** statement. An "else" statement is like a backup plan—if the condition in the "if" statement is not met, the computer will do something else instead. For example, you might not need an umbrella if it's not raining outside. In Python, you could use an "else" statement to tell the computer to print "Don't bring an umbrella" if it's not raining outside.

Lastly, we have the "elif" statement, which is short for **else**

if. An "elif" statement is used when you have more than two conditions to check. For example, you might want to wear shorts if it's hot outside. If it's cold outside, you might want to wear a coat. But if it's mild outside, you might want to wear a sweater. In Python, you could use an "elif" statement to tell the computer to print "Wear shorts" if it's hot outside, "Wear a coat" if it's cold outside, and "Wear a sweater" if it's mild outside.

Now that you know what each of them is, we can go ahead and take a look at some examples to understand how you would use them in your code. But first, let's take a look at a quick recap of each of these condition flow statements:

```
if condition: # code to execute if condition is true
```

```
else: #code to execute if all conditions are false
```

```
elif condition: #code to execute if the first condition is
false and this condition is true
```

If

The **if statement** executes a code block if a certain condition is true. Here's an example:

```
age = 10
if age > = 18:
    print("You can vote!")
```

In this example, the program checks if the value of the variable "age" is greater than or equal to 18. If it is, the message "You can vote!" is printed.

Else

The **else statement** is used to execute a block of code if the condition in the "if" statement is not true. Here's an example:

```
age = 10
if age > = 18:
    print("You can vote!")
else:
```

```
    print("You can't vote yet.")
```

In this example, the program checks if the value of the variable "age" is greater than or equal to 18. If it is, the message "You can vote!" is printed. Otherwise, the message "You can't vote yet." is printed.

Elif

The "elif" statement is used to check multiple conditions. If the first condition is not true, the program moves on to the next condition. Here's an example:

```
age = 10
if age > = 18:
    print("You can vote!")
elif age > = 16:
    print("You can drive, but you can't vote yet.")
else:
    print("You can't vote or drive yet.")
```

In this example, your program will check if the value of the variable "age" is greater than or equal to 18. If it is, the message "You can vote!" is printed. If the first condition is not true, then the program checks if the " age " value is greater than or equal to 16. If it is, the message "You can drive, but you can't vote yet." is printed. Otherwise, "You can't vote or drive yet." is printed.

Recap: Comparison Operators

To look at how these comparison operators can be used with flow statements, I have prepared four examples to recap the concept. Here they are:

Example 1:

```
number = 10
if number % 2 = = 0:
```

Python Coding for Kids

```
    print("The number is even.")
```

Here, the program checks if the number stored in the variable "number" is even by checking if it is divisible by 2 with no remainder. If it is, the message "The number is even." is printed.

Example 2:

```
password = "secret"
if password = = "secret":
    print("Access granted.")
```

In this example, the program checks if the value of the variable "password" equals the string "secret". If it is, the message "Access granted." is printed.

Example 3:

```
name = "Alice"
if name ! = "Bob":
    print("You're not Bob.")
```

For this code, the program checks if the value of the variable "name" is not equal to the string "Bob". If it is not, the message "You're not Bob." is printed.

Example 4:

```
fruits = ["apple", "banana", "orange"]
if "banana" in fruits:
    print("Bananas are in the fruit bowl.")
```

Finally, in the above illustration, the program checks if the list "fruits" contains the string "banana". If it does, the message "Bananas are in the fruit bowl." is printed.

Using Loops and Conditions With If Statements

When using conditional statements in Python, you can add them to loops and conditions with if statements to execute certain blocks of code multiple times or under different conditions. Although we have seen this previously, it is important to recap since this concept will be important to optimize your coding process.

Python's two main types of loops are **for** loops and **while** loops. "For" loops are used to execute a block of code a set number of times, while "while" loops are used to execute a block of code until a certain condition is no longer true. Shall we take a look at another example? Here, we are using a for loop with an if statement to print out all the even numbers between 1 and 10:

```
for i in range(1, 11):
    if i % 2 == 0:
        print(i)
```

In this example, the for loop goes through the values 1 to 10, and the "if" statement checks if each value is even. If it is, then the value is printed.

Finally, in this last example, I want to show you how to program a password into a program so that it will only open with the correct key. Remember this from before? Well, now is the time to see how this is done if you haven't already figured it out:

```
password = ""
while password != "secret":
    password = input("Enter the password: ")
    if password == "secret":
        print("Access granted.")
    else:
        print("Incorrect password. Try again.")
```

How about that? Now you can even password-protect what you create! In this example, the while loop keeps prompting the user to enter a password until they enter the correct one (which is the string "secret"). The if statement checks if the user's input equals the correct password and prints out either "Access granted." or "Incorrect password. Try again." depending on the input.

In both cases, the condition is a Boolean expression that evaluates to either true or false. If the condition is true, the code block indented underneath the "if" statement will be executed. If the condition is false, then the loop will continue to the next iteration (if using a "for" loop) or exit (if using a "while" loop).

Summary

In this chapter of the book, you have learned the final essential element to start developing your own programs in Python: conditional statements. When you place these together with the knowledge you have obtained from the previous chapters, you will see that there is a lot you can do. This means applying the if, else, and elif statements to direct your program to carry out the tasks you wish and establish the correct flow of operations. Let's go to the final set of assignments to ensure you understand everything.

Assignments

1. Write a program that asks the user to enter a number between 1 and 10. If the number is less than 5, the program should print "Too small." If the number is greater than or equal to 5 and less than or equal to 7, the program should print "Just right." If the number is greater than 7, the program should print "Too big.

2. Write a program that generates a random number between 1 and 100 and asks the user to guess the number. The program should tell the user if their guess is too high or too low and allow them to guess again until they guess the number correctly. The program should also keep track of the number of guesses it takes the user

to guess the number correctly and print out a message at the end.

3. Write a program that asks the user to enter a word. The program should print out the word, one letter at a time, and whether each letter is a vowel or a consonant.

4. Write a program that asks the user to enter a positive integer. The program should print out all the factors of the number.

5. Write a program that asks the user to enter a sentence. The program should count the words in the sentence and print out the total.

6. Write a program that asks the user to enter a positive integer. The program should print out whether the number is prime or not.

Challenge:

Write a program that generates a random word and asks the user to guess the word one letter at a time. The program should keep track of the number of incorrect guesses and print out a message if the user has exceeded a certain number of guesses.

Conclusion

Congratulations! You have reached the end of the book! How neat is it that you can now code and write programs in Python? You might not know this clearly yet, but in a world in which technology is gaining importance by the day, this will be an important asset to have in the future.

In this book, you have learned all about Python variables, data sets, and how to import and use modules—especially the Turtle module, that will enable you to create your own graphics. Cool, right? You have also seen how to use the if, else, elif statements and several other arithmetic and logical operators that offer many possibilities. Now all that you have to do is practice!

In addition, I am sure you have managed to get all the assignments—and maybe even the challenges—correct. Well done! If you haven't, there is no need to worry; go back to the chapters you have doubts about and re-read the information. You must follow each chapter by coding on your computer to have hands-on practice with coding and understanding the logic.

I suggest that you keep this book nearby and don't be afraid to look up answers to questions you might have. In addition to this, as I have mentioned before, you can also go online to the Python.org website and look at all the documentation they have. It is really easy to read and will give you a lot more new information.

I hope you enjoyed your journey, and I look forward to seeing what you can do! Good luck and great coding!

Answer Key

Here you will find all the answers for the assignments I have proposed throughout the book.

Chapter 2 Answers:

Assignment 1:

print("My name is Hansel, I am 12 years old and my favorite animal is a tiger")

Sample expected output:

My name is Hansel, I am 12 years old, and my favorite animal is a tiger.

Assignment 2:

name = "Hansel"

age = 12

favorite_animal = "tiger"

print(f"My name is {name}, I am {age} years old and my favorite animal is a {favorite_animal}")

Sample expected output:

My name is Hansel, I am 12 years old, and my favorite animal is a tiger.

Assignment 3:

print(f"My name is {name}, \n I am {age} years old and \n my favorite animal is a {favorite_animal}")

Sample expected output:

My name is Hansel, I am 12 years old, and my favorite animal is a tiger.

Assignment 4:

name = "Hansel"

age = 13

```
favorite_animal = "Rabbit"

print(f"My name is {name}, \n I am {age} years old and
\n my favorite animal is a {favorite_animal}")
```

Sample expected output:

My name is Hansel, I am 13 years old, and my favorite
animal is a Rabbit.

Challenge:

```
print("              (0)")
print("        (0)(0)(0)")
print("     (0)(0)(0)(0)(0)")
print("  (0)(0)(0)(0)(0)(0)(0)")
```

Chapter 3 Answers

Assignment 1:

```
side_length = 5
area = side_length ** 2
print(area)
```
Expected output: 25

Assignment 2:

```
item1 = 10
item2 = 20
item3 = 30
subtotal = item1 + item2 + item3
tax = subtotal * 0.08
total = subtotal + tax
print(total)
```
Expected output: 70.4

Assignment 3:

```
john_age = 25
jane_age = 30
is_john_younger = john_age < jane_age
print(is_john_younger)
```
Expected output: True

Assignment 4:

```
x = 7
print(x >= 5 and x <= 10)  # output: True
y = 3
print(y >= 5 and y <= 10)  # output: False
```
Expected output: True
                 False

Assignment 5:

```
x = 3 + 4 * 5
print(x)
```
Expected output: 23

Assignment 6:

```
x = (5 + 7) * 2
print(x >= 24)
```
Expected output: True

Assignment 7:

```
x = 10 / (5 * 2)
print(x)
```
Expected output: 1.0

Note that by putting the multiplication operation in parentheses, we ensure that it is performed before the division operation, which gives us a result of 1.0 instead of 4.0.

Challenge:

The calculation is done in the following order:

Parentheses: (8 + 2) = 10

Exponents: 4 ** 2 = 16

Multiplication: (12 / 3) * 10 = 40

Subtraction: 40 - 16 = 24

So the final result is 60.0.

Chapter 4 Answers

Assignment 1:

```
name = input("What's your name? ")
name = input("What's your name? ")
age = int(input("How old are you? "))
print("Hi,", name, "! You are", age, "years old.")
```

Assignment 2:

```
length = float(input("Enter the length: "))
width = float(input("Enter the width: "))
area = length * width
print("The area of the rectangle is", area, "square units.")
```

Assignment 3:

```
celsius = float(input("Enter the temperature in Celsius: "))
Fahrenheit = celsius * 1.8 + 32
print("The temperature in Fahrenheit is", fahrenheit, "degrees.")
```

Assignment 4:

```
birth_year = int(input("What year were you born? "))
current_year = 2023
age = current_year - birth_year
```

```
print("You are", age, "years old.")
```

Assignment 5:

```
kilometers = float(input("Enter the distance in kilometers: "))
miles = kilometers / 1.609
print("The distance in miles is", miles, "miles.")
```

Assignment 6:

```
name = input("What's your name? ")
color = input("What's your favorite color? ")
print(name + "'s favorite color is", color + ".")
```

Assignment 7:

```
base = float(input("Enter the base: "))
height = float(input("Enter the height: "))
area = 0.5 * base * height
print("The area of the triangle is", area, "square units.")
```

Challenge:

```
import math
radius = float(input("Enter the radius: "))
area = math.pi * radius ** 2
perimeter = 2 * math.pi * radius
print("The area of the circle is", area, "square units.")
print("The perimeter of the circle is", perimeter, "units.")
```

Chapter 5 Answers

Assignment 1:

```
for num in range(2, 21, 2):
print(num, end = ' ')
```

Assignment 2:

```
num = 1
total = 0
while num <= 100:
total += num
num += 1
print(total)
```

Assignment 3:

```
for i in range(1, 11):
print("5 x", i, "=", 5 * i)
```

Assignment 4:

```
num1, num2 = 0, 1
count = 0
while count < 10:
print(num1, end = ' ')
nth = num1 + num2
num1 = num2
num2 = nth
count += 1
```

Assignment 5:

```
total = 0
for num in range(1, 101):
if num % 3 = = 0:
total += num
print(total)
```

Assignment 6:

```
num = 2
count = 0
```

```
while count < 10:
for i in range(2, num):
if num % i == 0:
break
Else:
print(num, end = ' ')
count += 1
num += 1
```

Challenge

Here is a possible solution:

```
num = int(input("Enter a positive integer: "))
for i in range(1, num+1):
print("*" * i)
```

Explanation

First, the program prompts the user to enter a positive integer using the input() function and converts the input to an integer using the int() function, storing it in the variable num.

Then, a for loop is used to iterate through a range of numbers from 1 to num, using the range() function. The range() function generates a sequence of numbers starting from the first argument (inclusive) and ending at the second argument (exclusive), so range(1, num+1) generates the numbers 1, 2, 3, ..., num.

Inside the loop, the print() function is used to output a string of asterisks (*) multiplied by the loop variable i, which increases from 1 to num in each iteration of the loop. So in the first iteration, i is 1, and the program prints a single asterisk (*); in the second iteration, i is 2, and the program prints two asterisks (**), and so on, until the final iteration where i is num and the program prints num asterisks (*****).

Chapter 6 Answers

Assignment 1:

```python
import turtle
my_turtle = turtle.Turtle()
for i in range(4):
    my_turtle.forward(100)
    my_turtle.left(90)
turtle.done()
```

Assignment 2:

```python
import turtle
my_turtle = turtle.Turtle()
my_turtle.begin_fill()
for i in range(3):
    my_turtle.forward(100)
    my_turtle.left(120)
my_turtle.end_fill()
turtle.done()
```

Assignment 3:

```python
import turtle
my_turtle = turtle.Turtle()
my_turtle.circle(50)
turtle.done()
```

Assignment 4:

```python
import turtle
my_turtle = turtle.Turtle()
for i in range(5): #Draw a star
```

```
my_turtle.forward(100)
my_turtle.right(144)
turtle.done()
```

Assignment 5:
```
import turtle
my_turtle = turtle.Turtle()
for i in range(50): #Draw a spiral
my_turtle.forward(i * 10)
my_turtle.right(144)
turtle.done()
```

Assignment 6:
```
import turtle
my_turtle = turtle.Turtle()
for i in range(8): #Draw a snowflake
my_turtle.forward(50)
my_turtle.backward(50)
my_turtle.right(45)
my_turtle.right(90)
my_turtle.forward(50)
my_turtle.left(135)
for i in range(8):
my_turtle.forward(50)
my_turtle.backward(50)
my_turtle.right(45)
turtle.done()
```

Challenge:
```
Import turtle
```

```
import random
my_turtle = turtle.Turtle() #Create a turtle object
turtle.setup(400, 400) #Set the screen size
for i in range(100): #Draw a random walk
my_turtle.forward(10)
x = random.randint(-20, 20)
y = random.randint(-20, 20)
my_turtle.set heading(my_turtle.towards(x, y))
my_turtle.goto(x, y)
turtle.done()
```

Explanation: We use a loop to draw a random walk. The forward method moves the turtle forward by 10 units, and we use the random module to generate random values for the x and y coordinates of the next position. We use the towards the method to determine the turtle's heading toward the next position and then use the goto method to move the turtle to that position. The loop runs 100 times, so we get 100 random steps. The **turtle. The setup** function will set the size of the screen.

Chapter 7 Answers

Assignment 1:

```
num = int(input("Enter a number between 1 and 10: "))
if num < 5:
print("Too small.")
elif num >= 5 and num <= 7:
print("Just right.")
Else:
print("Too big.")
```

Assignment 2:

```
import random
```

```
num = random.randint(1, 100)
guesses = 0
While True:
guess = int(input("Guess the number between 1 and 100: "))
guesses += 1
if guess = = num:
print("Congratulations, you guessed the number in", guesses, "guesses!")
break
elif guess < num:
print("Too low. Guess again.")
Else:
print("Too high. Guess again.")
```

Assignment 3:

```
word = input("Enter a word: ")
vowels = "aeiouAEIOU"
For letters in words:
If the letter in vowels:
print(letter, "is a vowel.")
Else:
print(letter, "is a consonant.")
```

Assignment 4:

```
num = int(input("Enter a positive integer: "))
print("The factors of", num, "are:")
for i in range(1, num+1):
if num % i = = 0:
```

```
print(i)
```

Assignment 5:

```
sentence = input("Enter a sentence: ")
words = sentence.split()
count = len(words)
print("There are", count, "words in the sentence.")
```

Assignment 6:

```
num = int(input("Enter a positive integer: "))
is_prime = True
if num < 2:
is_prime = False
Else:
for i in range(2, num):
if num % i = = 0:
is_prime = False
break
if is_prime:
print(num, "is prime.")
Else:
print(num, "is not prime.")
```

Challenge:

```
import random
words = ["apple", "banana", "cherry", "orange", "grape",
"kiwi", "lemon", "mango", "pear", "pineapple"]
word = random.choice(words)
max_guesses = 7
incorrect_guesses = 0
letters_guessed = []
```

```
print("The word contains", len(word), "letters.")
While True:
guess = input("Guess a letter: ").lower()
If guess in letters_guessed:
print("You already guessed that letter. Try again.")
Else:
letters_guessed.append(guess)
If guess in word:
print("Correct!")
Else:
incorrect_guesses += 1
print("Incorrect.")
if incorrect_guesses = = max_guesses:
print("Sorry, you've run out of guesses. The word was",
word)
break
if set(word) = = set(letters_guessed):
print("Congratulations, you guessed the word", word, "!")
break
```

Here you will note that the code generates a random word from a list of words, sets a maximum number of guesses, and tracks the number of incorrect guesses and letters guessed by the user. For this example, the while loop allows the user to guess a letter at a time, and if the guess is correct, the program prints "Correct!" and if the guess is incorrect, the program increments the **incorrect_guesses** variable and prints "Incorrect.". The program also checks if the user has exceeded the maximum number of guesses and prints a message if the user loses. The program prints a congratulatory message if the user guesses all the letters correctly.

About the Author

Santos Ozoemena is a passionate Data Scientist, coder, and programmer. They are passionate about the art and the craft of being an expert coder and enthusiastic about teaching others how to code easily and effortlessly. With their countless years of studying data science, Python, and its information, they have gathered advanced knowledge of the field and its applications. To them, helping users achieve exceptional skills in programming matters deeply since what is learned will help the reader gain a serious, competitive edge in the job market

When they thought about writing a book, the first target audience they thought of was children because they believe it is important to learn these skills as early as possible. In addition, they have been in the same shoes as all beginner programmers and Data Scientists—with great curiosity and desire to learn. They understand the need to learn programming for the job market and want to help beginners reach a level of proficiency.

References

a-Rye. (n.d.). *Debugging*. CodingGame.
https://www.codingame.com/playgrounds/64843/begi
nner-python-concepts/debugging

Brewster, C. (n.d.). *16 examples of global companies using Python in 2022*. Trio Developers.
https://www.trio.dev/blog/companies-using-python

Dharmkar, R. (n.d.). *Where are the Python modules stored?*
Tutorials Point. https://www.tutorialspoint.com/Where-are-the-python-modules-stored

Introduction to Python: Functions Cheatsheet. (n.d.).
Codecademy.
https://www.codecademy.com/learn/flask-introduction-to-python/modules/learn-python3-functions/cheatsheet

Javatpoint. (n.d.). *Python print() function*.
https://www.javatpoint.com/python-print-function

OpenSource. (n.d.). *What is Python?*
https://opensource.com/resources/python

Pawandeep. (n.d.). *How to install Python in Windows?*
Tutorialspoint. https://www.tutorialspoint.com/how-to-install-python-in-windows

Python. (n.d.). *Lexical analysis*. Python.org.
https://docs.python.org/3/reference/lexical_analysis.ht
ml#identifiers

Python - Loops. (n.d.). Tutorialspoint.
https://www.tutorialspoint.com/python/python_loops.h
tm

Python - Tuples. (2019). Tutorialspoint.
https://www.tutorialspoint.com/python/python_tuples.h
tm

Python - Variables. (n.d.). Tutorialspoint.
https://www.tutorialspoint.com/python/python_variabl

es.htm

Python booleans. (n.d.). W3 Schools.
https://www.w3schools.com/python/python_booleans.
asp

*Python conditional statements: If_else, Elif, Nested If
Statement.* (2023, February 10). Software Testing Help.
https://www.softwaretestinghelp.com/python/python-
conditional-statements/

Python for loop. (n.d.). Programiz.
https://www.programiz.com/python-programming/for-
loop

Python loops. (n.d.). Javatpoint.
https://www.javatpoint.com/python-loops

Python reserved words list - Your complete guide. (n.d.).
Flexiple. https://flexiple.com/python/python-reserved-
words/

Python Software Foundation. (2019). *What is Python?*
Python.org. https://www.python.org/doc/essays/blurb/

Python Strings. (n.d.-a). CodesDope.
https://www.codesdope.com/course/python-string/

Python strings. (n.d.-b). W3 Schools.
https://www.w3schools.com/python/python_strings.asp

Python tuple (with examples). (n.d.). Programiz.
https://www.programiz.com/python-
programming/tuple

Python variables. (n.d.). W3 Schools.
https://www.w3schools.com/python/python_variables.
asp

Real Python. (n.d.). *Python 3 installation & setup guide.*
https://realpython.com/installing-python/

W3 Schools. (2019a). *Python Conditions.*
https://www.w3schools.com/python/python_conditions
.asp

W3 Schools. (2019b). *Python for loops.*
https://www.w3schools.com/python/python_for_loops.
asp

W3 Schools. (2019c). *Python print() function.*
https://www.w3schools.com/python/ref_func_print.asp

Turtle — Turtle graphics — Python 3.7.4 documentation. (2019).
Python.org. https://docs.python.org/3/library/turtle.html

Python module index — Python 3.10.7 documentation. (n.d.).
Python.org. https://docs.python.org/3/py-
modindex.html

GeeksforGeeks. (2016, May 27). *Tuples in Python.*
https://www.geeksforgeeks.org/tuples-in-python/

allisonf. (2017, February 15). *Effective debugging, with Python
and print statements.* Code Mentor.
https://www.codementor.io/@allisonf/how-to-debug-
python-code-beginners-print-line-du107ltvx

Reynolds, J. (2018, February 8). *8 world-class software
companies that use Python.* Real Python.
https://realpython.com/world-class-companies-using-
python/

Jablonski, J. (2018, May 14). *Python 3's f-Strings: An improved
string formatting syntax.* Real Python.
https://realpython.com/python-f-strings/

Campbell, S. (2019, October 23). *Python IF, ELSE, ELIF, Nested IF
& switch case statement.* Guru99.
https://www.guru99.com/if-loop-python-conditional-
structures.html

Rudick, M. (2020, January 5). *Python debug tools: More than
just a (print) statement.* Rookout.
https://www.rookout.com/blog/python-debugging-
more-than-just-a-print-statement/

Lathkar, M. (2020, February 14). *What are reserved keywords in
Python?* TutorialsPoint.
https://www.tutorialspoint.com/What-are-Reserved-

Keywords-in-Python

Silaparasetty, N. (2020, February 26). *The beginner's guide to Python Turtle*. Real Python. https://realpython.com/beginners-guide-python-turtle/

Elements, C. (2020, May 4). *Python for kids - Why Python language is perfect for kids?* Coding Elements. https://www.codingelements.com/blog/why-python-programming-language-is-perfect-for-kids

John, G. (2020, June 26). *Hexadecimal number system*. Tutorialspoint. https://www.tutorialspoint.com/hexadecimal-number-system

Amos, D. (2020, September 16). *Numbers in Python*. Real Python. https://realpython.com/python-numbers/#complex-numbers

Loeber, P. (2020, September 17). *How to use the Python Debugger using the breakpoint()*. Python Engineer. https://www.python-engineer.com/posts/python-debugger-and-breakpoint/

Tiwari, P. (2021, April 12). *How to learn Python for kids? Kid's guide to programming a robot using Python*. The Real School. https://therealschool.in/blog/how-learn-python-kids-guide-programming-robot-using-code/amp/

Moura, R. (2021, April 29). *Python IDLE debugger*. Renan Moura - Software Engineering. https://renanmf.com/python-idle-debugger/

Omisola, I. (2021, June 7). *How to debug your python code*. Make Use Of. https://www.makeuseof.com/debug-python-code/

Goyal, C. (2021, July 8). *Working with Modules in Python: Must know fundamentals for data scientists*. Analytics Vidhya. https://www.analyticsvidhya.com/blog/2021/07/workin

g-with-modules-in-python-must-known-fundamentals-for-data-scientists/

Tagliaferri, L. (2021, August 20). *Variables in Python 3: Naming style, reassigning, local & global*. DigitalOcean. https://www.digitalocean.com/community/tutorials/how-to-use-variables-in-python-3

Zaionce, B. (2021, August 27). *10 reasons why all kids should learn Python*. Code Monkey. https://www.codemonkey.com/blog/10-reasons-why-all-kids-should-learn-python/

Ddeevviissaavviittaa. (2021, August 28). *Python print() function*. GeeksforGeeks. https://www.geeksforgeeks.org/python-print-function/

Arora, N. (2021, October 6). *How to download and install Python latest version on Linux?* GeeksforGeeks. https://www.geeksforgeeks.org/how-to-download-and-install-python-latest-version-on-linux/

The Real School. (2022, March 29). *Is Python coding good for kids? Let's check out why should kids learn Python?* https://therealschool.in/blog/learn-python-coding-good-kids/

Chafi, R. (2022, May 20). *A comprehensive guide to Python modules*. Medium. https://python.plainenglish.io/a-comprehensive-guide-to-python-modules-db99bba37264

Yadav, O. (2022, October 5). *How to install Python on Mac and run your first script*. Make Use Of. https://www.makeuseof.com/how-to-install-python-on-mac/

GeeksforGeeks. (2022, October 13). *Python Modules*. https://www.geeksforgeeks.org/python-modules/

Co-Learner. (2022, November 19). *Download, setup & install Python on Windows*. Co-Learning Lounge. https://medium.com/co-learning-lounge/how-to-

download-install-python-on-windows-2021-
44a707994013

JetLearn. (2023, January 22). *Why Python is a great language to learn for kids.*
https://www.jetlearn.com/blog/python-is-great-for-kids

Campbell, S. (2023, January 23). *Python escape character sequences (examples).* Guru 99.
https://www.guru99.com/python-escape-characters.html

Python Land. (2023, January 31). *Install Python: Detailed instructions for Windows, Mac, and Linux.*
https://python.land/installing-python

Looping in Python (for, while, nested loops). (2023, February 8). Software Testing Help.
https://www.softwaretestinghelp.com/python/looping-in-python-for-while-nested-loops/

Biswal, A. (2023, February 10). *A beginner's guide to python variables.* Simplilearn.
https://www.simplilearn.com/tutorials/python-tutorial/python-variables

Gupta, A. (2023, February 10). *Top 10 Reasons why you should learn Python.* Simplilearn.
https://www.simplilearn.com/tutorials/python-tutorial/why-learn-python

Simplilearn. (2023, February 13). *The basics of Python loops.*
https://www.simplilearn.com/tutorials/python-tutorial/python-loops

Python data types. (2023, February 20). Software Testing Help.
https://www.softwaretestinghelp.com/python-data-types/

GeeksforGeeks. (2023a, February 28). *Turtle programming in Python.* https://www.geeksforgeeks.org/turtle-programming-python/

Shruthitv. (2023, March 10). *Python variables.* GeeksforGeeks.

https://www.geeksforgeeks.org/python-variables/

GeeksforGeeks. (2023b, March 14). *Loops in Python.*
https://www.geeksforgeeks.org/loops-in-python/

Sturtz, J. (2018a, April 17). *Python modules and packages – An introduction.* RealPython.
https://realpython.com/python-modules-packages/

Sturtz, J. (2018b, June 5). *Basic data types in Python.* Real Python. https://realpython.com/python-data-types/

Sturtz, J. (2018c, September 5). *Conditional statements in Python.* Real Python. https://realpython.com/python-conditional-statements/

Printed in Poland
by Amazon Fulfillment
Poland Sp. z o.o., Wrocław
10 October 2023

ae494e4c-6932-4cfb-b2b4-83c02c97cfd3R01